Forward

This is a book of poems I have written. I started writing them as an outlet. It was just a way of expressing my emotions. The challenge was to say what I wanted to say while keeping them in rhyme and try to make an even flow of words.

I began this with friends at a web site called 'AuthorsDen.com.' It became a passion. Many of the poems here are posted on my web site. Some I have saved for this book. The name, "Rebirth of the Dogwood" came from a true story. When my wife and I bought our home more than thirty-seven years ago there was a beautiful pink dogwood in the front yard. We thought we lost it a few years ago when it became sickly and stopped giving the wonderful blossoms. I reluctantly cut it down but left the stump. Ann said she would put a flower pot on it and we would have at least that to remember the tree by.

The tree didn't give up as easily as we thought. Two years later it began to send little trees coming off the root. It is now a bush but it is blossoming. We could turn it into a tree if we wanted to prune but I think I like it in the shape it is in. This gave me reason to wonder at the Majesty of God. Like the Dogwood, we will be reborn one day.

I hope you enjoy this book.
Sincerely,
Lew Duffey

Rebirth of the Dogwood

ISBN 978-0-6151-4491-7

Copyright:

2007, Lewis W Duffey Jr

Rebirth of a Dogwood

This book is a combination of thoughts and memories written either in prose or poetry. They come from a lifetime of living. That sounds like a redundancy, doesn't it? The fact is as we grow older we become aware of our youthful mistakes and pitfalls. They can either make us spend our so called golden years feeling guilty that we wasted so much of our youth or they can make us simply more aware of what our kids are facing. I must admit that life when I was a kid things seemed less tense and more carefree than my kids are dealing with today. I realize, though that this may simply be a point of view and is quite possibly due to the fact that it has been a long time since I was a kid.

Let me see if I can go back. I grew up in the forty's, fifties and sixty's. I graduated high school in 1963. I include the sixties as part of the time in which I grew up because, although I considered myself an adult the day I graduated from High School, I had not really done so yet.

During the fifties, I remember we were in the middle of the cold war. The Soviets were quite possibly going to drop a hydrogen bomb on us at anytime. We had drills at school teaching us what they called duck and cover drills. We would sit under our desk and keep our heads down and our eyes closed. Looking back I wonder how this was going to do anything during a nuclear attack. Be that as it may, we were drilled on safety measures to take if an all out war were to happen.

I truly believe that my faith in God was the one thing that kept me from simply giving up on it all and doing something crazy. The fact is I have probably done so on occasion in spite of his urging me not to do so. I talk to God and I ask of God but I have learned that this is not enough. I also have to listen to God. But speaking of prayer, I wrote this one because I felt compelled to give prayer a little praise. By doing so, I praise God.

I Pray

I pray for those who do not know my Lord

For they have somehow gone astray.

Jesus Christ is the living word

He lives for us and through us as we live each day.

His life is great and his forgiveness never fails

That's why I understand his gracious love

His spirit moves me like wind upon the sails

Of a ship that is guided by Gods son, the Dove.

Know his love and live it well

Know his peace that frees our burdened minds

Know words of joy that make our hearts swell.

Let our hearts not be confused and our eyes not be blind.

Over the years I have learned not to ask for so much from the Lord. After all did Jesus not tell us the father already knows what we need? Sometimes it is best to simply sing praises or carry on a conversation that says, "I love you, Lord. It also gives my own spirit a lift for by praising him I am reminding myself that there is someone there to pray to. I know someone who cares and someone who's taken my sin on his shoulders to pay the price for my transgressions. Hence, comes the next poem.

Strong Shoulders to Comfort Us

Lord, your shoulders carry a heavy load.
You hear my prayers both good and bad.
Still you lead me down the narrow road
You cry with me when I am sad
I lift my eyes up high to you
For strength to see me through each day
You help me do the things I do
And teach me how I ought to pray.
So my prayers to you both old and new
are from the heart and full of love that's true
Because Jesus Christ gives me faith and power
You help me over my weakest hour.

Do you remember what I said about those duck and cover drills we had when I was in school? I suppose they are nothing compared to what the people in the Middle East are going through right now. I must say, my prayers are for them all. I do not care what their religion is. That is between them and their maker so I will not judge.

I can only say that I have reached a point in my life when I feel like the cares of this world are not as great as I thought. After all, this life is temporary. I am praying for a life where peace is something that is an absolute. A place where everyone will share in a feeling of brotherhood and joy will prevail.

When I graduated high school I, like many other young men, joined the Army. I wasn't slated to go to Vietnam. I was going to Army finance school. That really blew my mind. The one subject that drove me crazy all through high school was math.

I would never make it that far. I was discharged from the Army five months and seventeen days after I went in. I did make it through basic training but I don't know how.

I spent two years in and out of the hospital while surgeons rebuilt my fallen arches and then I went into radio. I am sure this was something my Master was working with. The scriptures read all things work for the good of those who love the Lord. It didn't say all things good but rather all things.

My life became what it is today and even the unhappy times while in the Army walking painfully, causing many of the others call me things like "Hobby's Goat" or Hop-a-long skip-a-long and sometimes step and a half, were building blocks for my life. A life with memories I would not be willing to give up. Not even the bad ones for I have grown.

Jesus told us there would always be wars. He told us people would hate. But, he told us not to hate. The next poem speaks about the battle that goes on within us all

Good over Evil

Our world, you see can only be

If good can quiet the evil in you and me.

It is not Heaven we live in today

but it could be Hell where we will stay

if good does not disqualify

Horrors that are constantly floating by.

God gives us forgiveness and wonderful grace

without which you and I cannot face

His love and goodness given throughout time

for without his love this is just a rhyme.

But let us know that Good survives

Without it our soul grows weak and dives
Into blackness from which we cannot free
Ourselves because we simply cannot see
The tree was cut down and we missed not its leaves
Until we found there was no breeze
And we could not breathe because you see
We breathe the oxygen from the tree.
So think before your axe destroys
remembering that when you hear the horrible noise
of a dying tree,
it will soon be the end of you and me.
Satan's biggest success in this world today
Is making us believe he does not exist.
This makes us lose our convictions making it easier to stray
From the true word of God, making us to weak to resist
the sin of omission for we lose the faith we need each day
Forgetting that Christ died for all of us high upon the cross
So that poor souls like you and I may never found that we're lost.
We must not give up our faith in God or in his only son
For the loss of faith in Jesus Christ would surely be our loss.
Praise God I say and Praise him in deed and sing
praises to his only son, our King.
When our earthly lives is done, our praises will never cease to ring.

Today we live in a world of technology. We send emails back and forth to people who we have never met and yet, we feel like we have made friends. This is good but there is something we need to keep in mind. With all its comforts and all our wonderful gadgets we are still missing something if we don't know God's email address. That would be JesusChrist.com. I have had several operations done to keep me here on earth but although I do thank the doctors for their work, I also praise God for the doctors.

There is a doctor's office in my town that has a picture that I would love to have but I can't even find a print of it online. A team of doctors are gathered around a patient on the operating table. Standing there beside them with his hand outstretched as if guiding the surgeon with the scalpel is Jesus, dressed in white. It is a wonderful and comforting picture.

Each time I had open heart surgery performed on me, I found myself wanting to ask God for protection but my heart knew he already knew what I needed. I found myself reciting the 23rd. Psalm. That's right, the one that starts out, "The Lord is my shepherd."

It helped me remind myself that no matter what happened I would not be separated from him. We all have mountains like this to climb. Some are higher than others and some valleys are deeper. That is what I was thinking about when I wrote the next poem.

The Mountain
I saw a mountain standing tall and high
I ask the Lord to move it aside.
The mountain stayed and I wondered why.
So I ask my Lord to make it hide.
He said my child, I will do something more.
I will not move the mountain but give greater faith so you will dare
to climb the mountain that leads to Heavens door.
You will know such joy that you will no longer care
That the mountain was ever standing there.

We have all climbed those mountains. Jesus said if you have the faith the size of a mustard seed you can move mountains. However, he also said we would have days when we would feel sad or lonely. He never really promised to move mountains. The first question we need to ask is if it is his will that the mountain is moved. We too often ask God for things, comforts, love or even earthly riches. We should ask for eternity in his arms.

I Asked for Love

I asked God to give me comforts to fill my life with joy
He said, "Take comfort in your faith and live it day by day.
I asked God to ease my pain of problems that annoy.
He said, "If you felt no pain, you could not grow that way."
I begged the Father to give me peace so I'd never want to cry.
He told me that my tears were not the problem for they could easily be
wiped away.
I said, "Dear Lord, please give me riches so I will never sigh
'I know not what tomorrow brings be it feast or famine I cannot say.'
His answer was a resounding 'no' but he quickly explained why.
He said, "The riches you will never lose are those not of this world you
live in today.
True riches to you, my child are a life eternally with me up high.
No man can take that away from you
You need only to reach for me.
I will swipe you up into my arms, that's all I need to do
And you will know love for eternity for these are true riches, you see.
At this point I stopped searching for things to ask my God to do.
I simply said, "I love you Lord for you have graciously taught me
That money cannot buy your love, no matter how I try.
You give it freely for you choose me and now your love I will not deny.

If you have kids, you really know the frustration of having one of them
hanging onto your leg because they want you buy candy at the store and you
said,

"You have had enough for one day." They will throw temper tantrums and may even shout, "I hate you." They don't mean it. They simply are too young to realize what hate is. They are simply frustrated. This is why as a parent we need to be patient with them. They learn from us, you know. They will learn patience by watching us. They can also learn impatience or even hatred if they see us show these destructive attitudes. That is why it is important for us not only to preach what we believe but live it. Read this next poem.

Patience

I asked the Lord for patience,
He gave me sorrow and pain.
I asked the lord for greater strength,
He gave me calluses to my disdain.

I asked the Lord to give me peace,
I find none on the Earth.
I asked the Lord to give me hope,
He did with his son's birth.

I asked the Lord for a closer walk
With his son to lead the way.
My prayers are nothing more than talk
If when he leads, I find I stray.

I find I ask for more and more
But do I ever give
To the one who suffered wounds so sore?
So that I may live?

Why do I not say "Thank you, Lord
For all the gifts you give

And promise not to ask for more
Than I need each day to live.

For Christ has taken on my sin
And he paid the price for me.
Why do I pray for Earthly Things?
And not for eternity?

If you are a regular at your church, you have sat through many
communion services. Some go to the alter to receive the communion. Others
have church deacons bring the communion to them. It doesn't matter either
way. What is important is that we know what the communion symbolizes,
the body and blood of our Lord, given for our eternal souls.

This is My Body, this is my blood.

"Take, eat. This is my body, broken for you."
This Jesus said to the twelve.
"I will hang high on the cross. It is this I must do
If I do not, you will find only sin in which to dwell.
They will curse me and hurt me for you my good friends
They will give me only vinegar to wet my lips as they chap and swell.
I will drink of the poison until it all ends
I will suffer from the nails, the cross and the whips thereby defeat the
powers of Hell.
I will do it to wipe away all of your sins
If I do not you will surely never find your way home
You will suffer and die after you find no peace where ever you may
roam."
He said to them then, "This is my blood which you drink.
This I gladly will shed for you.

With each swallow I ask you simply to think
Of my love and what it can do
To lift you above the cares of this world where you live
And stand you firmly in faith by Heavens gate.
I will help you to share the love that I give
To save others before it's too late."
He came for us and he died for us all.
God lifted him up from the dead.
Thereby lifting us up so we would never fall
We are the body, our Lord is the head.
Praise him now and praise him loud
Singing those praises to his name each day
Be humble and loving and never too proud
Kneel down before him and pray.

One of the joys of growing older is memories of watching your own children grew and mature. Another is grandchildren. I have five now. I have four grandsons and one granddaughter. It is always great to see them. Please forgive me for admitting this but the really great thing about grandchildren is spoiling them rotten and then sending them home.

We grow out of our childhood. This is a part of life but we really should keep some of the faith and some of the astonishment that we experienced as children.

Since we are on the subject, I want to share something of my childhood with you. I grew up in a small town. We most times did not have enough players for a baseball team so we used our imagination. We called it high fence over.

You see, it works like this. The ball field where a community adult ball team played had an extremely short left field. Only about two hundred and eighty feet down the left field line. Because homeruns would simply be too easy, they extended the fence out to where left field met center field, making it higher. We used that as our playing area.

It meant running the bases backwards so third base became first base and we were just kids so we were not going to run the entire 90 feet to the base. We put them closer.

Now this means the first baseman played at what should be the third base. If we had enough players we may have a short stop. If not the short stop and second baseman's position was covered by one player. We had a pitcher of course but no catcher. So if the batter missed the ball or decided not to swing he would be the one to run back to the backstop and fetch the ball, throwing it out to the pitcher.

I loved to play the game but I was never very good at it. I only ever hit one homerun that actually cleared that fence. My friends would not let me forget that it probably would not have been a home run if a storm the night before had not caused a limb to fall off a tree on the other side and thus cause the fence to collapse. They insisted the ball would not have cleared the twelve foot fence but I held onto the idea that this was my homerun. The reason I am really telling this story is to make a point that has nothing to do with the homerun. We had to make do with what we had. Too often I think as adults we forget the wondrous things that children can do when they need to. We played baseball, backwards all summer, every summer.

The Little Children

Take heart little children for you sins are forgiven in Christ's holy
name
And now, little children, abide in him and you will never need to feel
shame.

My Little children let us not love in word or tongue but in truth and
deed.
Let us be there for our brother when he finds that he is in great need.

Jesus spoke unto the crowd about the children he held dear

He told them that if they abide in him the Kingdom of God is near.

Except ye be as children he said, ye shall not enter Heavens gate
Lay your sins upon his shoulder before it is too late

Whosoever therefore shall humble himself as this little child, he said
Will never die but truly I say have eternal life instead

And who whoever shall receive one such little child in my holy name
Receives me also, to wash away his past, his sin and his shame

So come ye all to Christ in gracious and grateful love
Knowing that the joy you have comes from God Above

And never forget that Jesus said these words to you and me
If you only believe as a little child, Heavens Gates are just beyond the
sea.
Love one another.

Jesus once said, "If you have faith the size of a mustard seed you could ask anything of the Heavenly Father and it would be done. I truly believe Jesus laid hands on the sick and healed them but today we have doctors who help with that. I really don't think it is a lack of faith if I ask to be healed and am not. I think the lack of faith is asking. If I truly trust in him I know he already knows what I need. Therefore, I simply pray for the faith to live day by day no matter what it brings. He knows my aches and pains and he knows what I have need of. Why should I try to tell him what he already knows? It is clear to me that many times God know more about what I need than I do.

Why did you not give me the mustard Seed?
Why did you not answer my prayers Dear Lord?
Why did you not give it to me?
Why were you not true to your word?
You said, "What you ask, I will give to thee."
I only wanted the faith of a mustard seed.
I wanted to move that mountain aside.
I asked for no more than the faith I need
To move the mountain so high and wide.
You have chosen to withhold my faith, Dear Lord
I only asked you why this is so.
But, then you answered, "I was true to my word.
The mustard seed is planted and ready to grow.
You must remember My Son that a mustard seed,
Will not grow into an oak tree or a pine.
You will always receive whatever you need
So, ease your troubled mind.
That mountain was meant to stand proudly there,
So proud and long and tall.
It serves to protect you from the winds that trouble the air
It stands like a protecting wall.
And it's there especially for you to climb
From atop you will see the beauty of winter, spring, summer and fall.
And grow closer and closer to me all the time.
So I ask you," he said as I stood there before him.
"Do you really want it moved into the sea?
Would you not rather pray for strength to climb to its rim?
And see all its glory and commune with me
Where the view is so wonderfully great to see?"

As I grow older my mortality becomes more apparent. I know that no man is meant to live forever on this Earth. My eternity will be spent with God. I wonder, though if it might not be possible for my spirit to stay with those I love, giving comfort and company and continued friendship. It would be Heaven if I could come back as an Angel of my Lord and be their source of comfort. I know not what Heaven is. I only know it is wonderful.

We have all lost a loved one. My Mom died at the age of fifty-four, taken by cancer. My Dad lived till he was seventy-four. What I remember after my Mothers death was that Dad kept the house exactly as it was when she was there. Not even an ash tray was moved out of place. Eventually, he found another and remarried. She would be the first to tell you that they loved each other but Dad never stopped loving my mother. I think this next poem came from that.

Tears that Cleanse

She smiled but I could see in her eyes

A glassy stare and brimming tears

The fact that she smiles was no surprise

It was the tears she shed that cultured my fears.

"How may I help you," I begged of her then.

In spite of her pain she gave me a smile.

She said very quietly, "I know not where to begin."

Our love has been a growing together for quite a while

But I fear that it cannot overcome the test of time

For as we grow older we feel life quietly slip away

It gives no clue, no reason or rhyme.

We will be parted I know not what day

However I still get the blues, yes I do

Because we will be parted and I won't have you.

I held her and comforted her as best as I could

I assured her that our love is a love carved in wood

And that even from beyond my very own grave

There would be a private road of gold that we now pave
With each kiss we kiss and each hug that we give.
Our love will surely forever continue to live
Long after our flesh has turned cold we will Love
That love was given to each of us by God up above.

Our kids are trying to raise their families in a time when it is next to impossible with the cost of living skyrocketing. That is why my wife and I have had the grandchildren much of time, babysitting for our daughters while they work.

It can be tiring and I am not as young as I used to be but I would not trade the moments spent with any of them for all the money in the world. I see them learn, experiment and just plain fiddle with things. Their face can be a mixture of curiosity, complete joy and sometimes tears but they are always easy to love. I guess that is what I was thinking when I wrote the following poem because our ceiling fan seemed to attract the minds and imaginations of each of them.

Through The Eyes of a Baby

It goes around in a circle that never ends.
His eyes are drawn to its constant motion
Which mesmerizes him as it creates the winds
Into a breeze like that which blows off the ocean?
His eyes try to keep up as he is drawn into its world of spins
He doesn't seem to notice the air that it sends
But he sees how it moves as it creates its cool winds.
He is only a baby; he knows not what it's for
Nor does he care that the air feels soft and cool
His mind is caught up in its wonderful allure
He doesn't know now that's its movements can rule
His mind and his spirit as it spins above.

Before his eyes close and he notices no more
I look at him as he sleeps my bundle of love.
I lay him down gently as I close the door.
I sing chorales of praises to my God up above.

Have you ever felt like God has forsaken you? It's not that uncommon. Even Jesus felt it. He cried out from on the cross, "why hath thou forsaken me?" Of course it took the cross to make him cry out. Our faith is not as strong. We need his constant reassurance to make it through each day.

I Am!

I prayed to God for comfort for I felt alone and empty.
I prayed for words from Heaven, Words that would serve to reassure me.
I prayed to feel the touch of his hand gently resting on my shoulder
I prayed God would give me eternal life but, alas I just grew older.
I prayed to God and Prayed to God for some signal from above
I only asked for reassurance that I could know his love.
His silence cut through me like a knife and seemed to drive my soul asunder.
I tried to grasp his hand in mine to comfort me through the lightning and the thunder.
Then one fine day I realized why God had kept so still.
He was allowing me to search for him and learn to understand his will.
For he does not promise earthly riches, comforts or even peace on earth
What he offers we must find or we will never know its worth.
I ask of God and ask of God but I never really knew his ways

One day, I asked no more of God, but promised to live for him through
all my days.
I would love the Lord with all my heart and love my neighbor and my
friends
I found that his love is eternal love which means it never ends.

Did you ever have one of those days? You know what I mean. It's a
day when Murphy's Law rules. Anything that can possibly go wrong will.

I could probably write a whole book on this subject if it were not for
the fact that this old man's memory isn't what it used to be.

I can remember one story that would be funny if it hadn't happened
to me. I used to suffer from seizures. The doctor put me on medication
which stopped the grand mall seizure but it created little mini- seizures. For
instance, one day I was setting at my table at an Optimist club luncheon
when I felt that creepy feeling moving over me. The next thing I knew I was
being confronted by a member of the cooking staff in the kitchen.

"Sir, you you're not allowed to be here," he said. I didn't want to
admit that I suffered from those things so I sort of stammered and asked
where the restroom was. The poor man had to show me although I had been
here many times and would usually know where the restroom was. Life is
like that. If you want perfection, you'll have to wait on the next life. This
one is anything but.

Life's Up's and Down's

What goes up must come down or so the scientists say
If you through a rock high in the air it will never, ever stay.
It will soon come plummeting down to Earth as gravity's force ordains
There upon the ground it lies and there it still remains
Until someone picks it up again and throws it way up high.
But alas, it only returns once more too quickly with a sigh.
Our life can be best explained that way to me it certainly seems

That we spend as much time on the ground looking back on unfulfilled
dreams.
But, if we pick ourselves up again and dare once more to try to fly
We experience the joy of living life and dare to touch the sky.
And if we should only find ourselves lying on the ground once more
We still have the wonderful knowledge that we flew to Heavens door.
So never give up when things get hard and never fear to live
And always remember that the joy received is proportional to what
you give.
As long as God breathes the breath of life into your body here on Earth
Live everyday with all your heart and never forget its worth.

So, I had seizures when I was young. I still take the medication. I also
had a heart attack at the age of forty. When I tell people this, they will say
that's much too young. Try telling that to my heart. I have had some
operations. Things have not always been glorious but I have also had more
thrills and blessings than I can count. My family, every one of them, is a
perfect example. Memories fade but some simply will not go away. I thank
God for that!

Look for the Silver Lining

So, the sun did not come out this day.

The sky is dark and moist and gray

You fear this day will bring us rain

So what is the reason for your disdain?

The rain is a vital part of living

It takes away nothing, it is intent on giving

Wonderful life to all and good health as well

The rain helps make the plants to grow and swell

Into wonderful green and beautiful fulfillment

Giving marvelous life to the entire environment.

Then the rays of the sun along with the rain can bring

Out the flowers about whose wonderful beauty we all love to sing.

So be not dismayed by the cool and rainy days

Let not your souls be shrouded or feel lost within the haze

Of the cool rainy weather for it is all a major part

Of the life that you and I both live which will soon warm the heart.

Come rain or come shine, it really makes little matter

They both add to life so let us not be the sadder

To see the rainy days appear as you know they surely will and do.

For they come to water the beautiful flowers that blossom and live for

me and for you.

In 1997 the world lost a wonderful woman. Mother Teresa died of a heart attack. She has been called the saint of the little things. In fact she once said,

"Little things are indeed little, but to be faithful in little things is a great thing." She also was quoted as saying the following: "If you can't feed a hundred people, then feed just one."

We should all live like that. Mother Teresa once said,

"When a poor person dies of hunger, it has not happened because God did not take care of him or her. It has happened because neither you nor I wanted to give that person what he or she needed."

Every little act of kindness that we show to our neighbor is recorded in Heaven. I don't know if Mother Teresa ever said that but I did.

The Little Things

Each small breath we breathe each beat of the heart
Are wondrous miracles and as such are a part
Of life's miraculous beauty, of life's marvelous drive
They help take us to a world of fulfillment for which we all strive.
We needn't worry where our life cometh from for that is ordained
For each breath we have taken has always remained
In the hands of the father who gives us our breath
Each breath we take sustains us and keeps us from death.
So, why do we worry about our future on earth?
Why do we not live life for all that its worth?
God gives us the heartbeat that keeps us alive.
He gives us the courage so we all can survive
Life's problems and troubles and still live each day
Believing in God so we honestly can say
I know not what the future holds but I know who is my guide
He is the one that I proudly call my God
He gave me my breath so with it I shout
Serving my Lord is what life's all about.
My Lord Jesus Christ has come into my being
And now I can walk through the dark without even seeing
For I know his light will guide me all the way
Each little breath I take as I live throughout my day.
Tomorrow is promised but I know not where I will be
But I care not, for wherever I am so is he.

While we are talking about little things I would like you to consider this. Why is it that a smile is so contagious? When you greet a friend or a stranger with a smile, the odds are great that you will get a smile in return. God's love makes us smile. Maybe it is that love conveyed through that smile that causes the smile that comes back.

The Miracle of a Smile

When I was no more than a child, you see
A smile from Mom or Dad meant the world to me.
As I grew older I met a girl so fair
I found her smile would make me stop and stare.
One day she blessed me with a baby boy
Again I found his smile caused so much joy.
Then came a girl and then another.
I cherished their smiles along with their brother and their mother
I found their smiles made my life fulfilled
My troubles would seem so small and be stilled
My happiness was built upon their love,
A love that originated from God above.
One by one they have brought grandchildren into my life
And I find that even amongst life's worries, cares and strife
There is great joy to be found in each tiny smile
A smile, you see never goes out of style
And it always seems to make me happy
The call me Papa instead of Pappy
But what they call me is not my fulfillment
Their smiles are my greatest and happiest endearment.
So Smile and watch as you see a smile reflected
A friendly smile is seldom rejected.

This thought has been with me for a long time. I probably have been considering it since I was a child. Why did God put that fruit tree in the Garden of Eden if he truly did not want Adam and Eve to partake of it? Would it have not been better if he just didn't put it there or if he built a wall around it so they could not get to it? I have no special knowledge here but I surmise that God knew what they would do. He also knew that even this first sin of man would bring about something that he could use to make them stronger.

The fruit tree was a test and I would suppose we would say that Adam and Eve failed the test. Therefore, we have to keep taking the test in one way or another until we have passed it. That is when Heavens Gate will open to us.

The Forbidden Fruit

Did our Heavenly Father truly think that Adam and Eve would not partake?
The fruit that he said was forbidden, that eating was a big mistake?
Did he really think that they would simply say, "I will not break his command?
Or did he know that once they knew it was forbidden it would be in great demand?
Did our Heavenly Father really make such a huge mistake?
Did he not know that surely they would feel compelled to partake?
Of the forbidden fruit that he loudly said, "you are not to touch."
Did he not know that such a demand would simply be too much?
He knew I believe that they would be compelled to eat that fruit for sure.
He knew that the sins would produce hardships that they would surely endure.
He placed that fruit for them to eat and thereby started a path
Of sin and doubt, of mistakes and wrongs, enough to cause his wrath.

Why did he put that fruit there? A question you may ask.
Was it not a costly, mistake and a useless task?
I tell you he put it there for them to eat and here is the reason why.
It was the first mistake of man and leads to more for you and I.
God knows we only grow in faith by learning from our mistakes
Realizing we have finally learned that we have done wrong is often
what it takes
To bring us closer to the Lord and make us want to grow and we must
By our mistakes we are made stronger and only then can we say "In
God We Trust."

Someone once wrote, "I would rather live as if there were a God only to die finding there was none than to live as if there were no God and find myself standing before him."

God has made himself as a mystery to us. Jesus came as the sign of his love for us but much of what or who God is escapes our feeble minds. We would like to say we've seen him but Jesus once said none have seen the father and lived. Moses saw a burning bush; others saw Angels sent from God. Our knowledge of our creator is based on faith. Without that we have nothing.

Without Faith

People hurry to and fro from place to place and keep the pace.
They seldom take time to stop and pray as they hurry through each
and every day.
They have work to do and bills to pay as each day comes and goes as if
in a race
They are busy and sometimes have little time to kneel and pray,
To say a thank-you to their Lord and God who watches as they go
about their chores.

It's sad because he hears no praise, no words of joy do they have time
to say.
The sadist thing about their plight is that they don't reach for Heavens
doors.
They seem to forget Gods almighty love and devotion
They get caught up in worry, anger and other destructive emotion.
So fall ye not into this trap from which it is so hard to pull free.
Each day say, "Thank you Lord for I know you truly love me."
Then live your life as if you truly want to give
That same love, compassion and the gift to forgive
Any one who may wrong you and hurt you in any way.
Live and love for God and your brother today.

You have heard the saying, "today is the first day of the rest of your life" I am sure. It means whatever your past you can start anew with each day and build your ability to love and inspire others to love.

For the sake of argument, let's say yesterday I had a bad day. I said something that hurt someone I loved or I went astray in some other way. Let's say I let my anger get the best of me. I awake this morning and I realize that one of the first things I need to do is apologize to God and to whichever person I may have offended. An apology is not that hard to say. Try it.

"I'm sorry!" There, that wasn't so hard was it? Now get on with your life and remember that our Heavenly Father promised to forgive and he will. He may ask for that apology, not because he needs it but because you do.

Each day begins a new chapter in the book of life. Each day offers a chance start over again and each day allows you to review your past and use the experience to make yourself stronger for the future.

Today is the First Day!

Today is the first day of the rest of your life.
Your tomorrows will bring many joys and some strife.
But there is one thing you should never fail to see
That is that god will be with you and he will also be with me.
Yesterday is but a memory of what has come and past
Today will be yesterday, yes it has a short time to last.
Tomorrow is a question as to what it will bring
Be it great joy or harsh pain, whether it will tickle or sting
We know not which, we will live it whatever it may be
What it will hand us when it comes we today cannot see.
But there is one absolute of which we are assured.
Whatever tomorrow brings we will be enforced by our Lord.
So take no time to worry or contemplate tomorrow.
Don't let yourself worry whether it brings happiness or sorrow
For God and his son Jesus Christ are yesterday, today and tomorrow.
So live your life today and always try to be your best
And when tomorrow comes then it will be today
As will the next and then the next until with God calls your soul will
rest.
Then for all eternity you will be held in his loving arms and there you
will stay.

I have memories of when I was a boy. I remember summer nights when lightning and thunder put on an extravagate show and I was the audience. My Mom was always a little afraid of the lightning but somehow I saw it as a beautiful presentation put on by God above. I say God above but as I grew older I began to realize that God is not just above. He is above, below and within us all. We are made in the very image of God. Yet, we are only a small part of what God is. The lightning is a wonderful reminder of his awesome power. I hope you enjoy the next poem:

Thunder and Lightning

I hear the rumble ringing through the night.
I see the streak of flashing light.
It makes the clouds glow all around
As again I hear that rumbling sound
The rain falls harsh and splashes high
As once more the lightning aluminates the sky.
There are those who fear this cosmic charge
The sound so loud and the lightning so large
But I watch it as a little child with wondrous eye
As I would watch fireworks of the fourth of July.
It puts on a marvelous and glorious show
As the lightning streaks jump to and fro.
The thunder comes from every side
The lightning makes no attempt to hide
Itself from my curious eye
The storm brings rain from up on high
Our Heavenly Father is like that you see?
He is always there for you and me
Be not afraid to hear his voice so clear
His brilliance gives us nothing to fear.
He is pure and never dying love!
That is why his Son was called the Dove.

If God Washed his Hands

My wife had a CD playing today for our grandson. It is a group of gospel songs sung by little children. They sing it with such innocence and passion that I found myself singing along.

One song gave me pause to think. It is a song I sang when I was a kid in Church. "He's got the Whole World in His Hands." It is a wonderful description of God's love for us all. The thought that came to mind has been playing with my mind ever since. That is why I needed to vent it so I decided to write about it.

Over the many millions of years that God has patiently worked to try to make us more loving and kind only to watch us allow hate drive us into crimes, war and many other forms of bigotry it would not be surprising if many times throughout history God has been tempted to wash his hands of the whole thing.

In a manner of speaking he did with the great flood. Only Noah and his family survived that one.

God has watched patiently as even the great ones like Moses and King David went astray. How many times has he had to forgive you and me? I am sure I have been the recipient more times than I deserve. Yet, he keeps waiting and working to help us realize our spiritual potential.

If you have read the bible as many times as I had even before I was out of grade school, you know that the Ten Commandments are not a cake walk. Jesus came to relieve us of some of the burden but he also made some more demands.

For instance, he said if we hate our brother we are guilty of murder in our heart, or at least we should be accountable. If we look at a woman with lust we are already are guilty of adultery in our hearts. He said that when we do not forgive another who has wronged us we have no reason to believe God will forgive us. If we do not feed the hungry we have not done this for him. As Jesus put is, "do unto others as you would have them do unto you."

We are all a little upset sometimes with our leaders in Washington. They make many promises to get us to vote them into office and then swiftly forget the promises and do what they want once they are in power.

The fact of the matter is this. We are not much better if we turn away from someone in need without trying to help in some way. We all find it very easy to turn our heads and look the other way.

We are taught as followers of Christ to welcome the poor with open arms. As Jesus said it, "for some have entertained Angels unawares." "As you have not done it to one of the least of one of these, you have not done it unto me." "Some have entertained Angels unawares." These are two poignant statements from the Master.

We must keep in mind that God gave his only begotten Son that whosoever believeth in him should not perish but have everlasting life. The question arises, what does this have to do with acts of kindness or the lack of forgiveness on our part?

Those acts are like milestones. If you cannot forgive, if you do not feel compelled to do good to those less fortunate than you, you do not believe in him.

What then, if I follow the Ten Commandments, if I do good deeds, if I forgive others who have wronged me, this is my ticket to heaven? NO! Actually these things come because we have accepted Jesus Christ and because we have confessed our sins and are constantly aware of our need for his love, help and yes, forgiveness.

You can't put the cart before the horse. The works come as a labor of love for the one who paid the price for our sins. The works earn nothing; they simply reflect our wondrous love for our maker.

In other words, if you are trying to earn your way into Heaven, you will find the door closed. If you simply learn to love the Lord thy God with all thy heart and all thy soul and thy entire mind, the works simply become as natural as breathing.

Let us all take some time to reflect on our lives and never cease to try to know him better.

With all this in mind, let your heart beat to the rhythm of this next poem. I wrote it because I truly believe many of us are tempted by the promise of a Heavenly life and allow that to create our reason for doing those good deeds. When we follow his way with the desire for a reward, we have not done it for the reason that brings real inner peace.

These Little Things, too

Do you love your brother or sister so they will love you?

Do you feed the poor for praises for what you do?

Do you serve God for eternal glory and praise?

Is it your wish for greater blessings throughout your days?

If you love your brother, that is good for it is God's will.

However, if you love him for your own salvation God's voice will be still.

You should want to serve god but not to achieve eternal life

Or to assure that you will not ever need to deal with troubles or strife.

The greatest blessing you can achieve in this life my friend

Is the blessing of the giving of love that knows no end?

God knows your mind and he also knows your heart.

He sent Jesus Christ to give us our start

But he is waiting on us to unselfishly love

And to reflect the greater love that comes from above.

So my friend I ask you why you serve God on high

Who sits on his thrown watching over you and I.

Is it to achieve salvation where time has no place?

Or is it because you have met your lord face to face?

Love your neighbors, do good to everyone you meet

Your salvation is already bought for you, a gift that is so sweet.

But do what you do out of true love for God and his son

And when you meet him again, he will praise what you've done.

Let God be the one who gives you the praise

He sees who you've helped and he counts the ways

That you have shown your love and your true commitment.

Not done to earn salvation for that has already been sent.

Love because God loved you first.

My life has been a collage of troubles, blessings and some periods of questioning on my part. Now as I look back I realize that if I changed anything about my past, even the bad things, I would not know my Heavenly Father as I do. Please do not get me wrong. I have not been the most wonderful follower he has. I have gone my own head-strong way too many times. What I am is forgiven. His love worked through even the bad parts of my life for my eternal salvation and if I walk away from that, I have only myself to blame for what may happen.

Every experience I have had in my life, both good and bad have been building blocks.

Building Blocks

The child sat upon the living room floor placing building blocks way up high.

As he looked down at the bottom he let out a long and lonely sigh.

All the other blocks were red but this one block was black.

He said to himself, "How can I let that block there in my red stack?

I will remove the block and replace it with a block that is red.

So he carefully pulled out that one black block and cried out when he did

Because as soon as he pulled the block away the others blocks tumbled
down
And where he once had a tower there was now blocks strewn around.
The child never gave a thought of what might happen when the block
was gone
He never thought that all the blocks depended upon this black one.
He tried once more to build his tower with red blocks and that was all
But the block he got to replace the black one was too large and it made
the tower fall.
Sometimes just as that little child, our lives are not always good.
But where we stand today depends upon the path upon which we have
stood.
If we change those painful, unhappy times that we all have had
We may find only that our future will turn out twice as bad.
So, my friend if you see something bad about the way you lived
yesterday
Simply pray to God through Jesus Christ and forgiveness will come
your way.
Learn from yesterday's mistakes and press on for tomorrow
To change the past may do nothing more than bring to you more
sorrow.

You read about God in books or see and hear his voice in the movies. His voice is like thunder. I challenge you to listen for God when he is not speaking loud. Sometimes his voice is nothing more than a whisper. Hence, my next poem:

My next poem sort of reverts back to the last. What we too often do not know is that God is building those blocks even when we think he has abandoned us. The fact is, sometimes these are the times when he working harder for us. Moreover, he is working all around us, all the time.

Where is God?

So many people have asked a question that burns into their spirit.
If there be a God why do I not see him and if he has a voice why do I
not hear it?
The answer is simple but often overlooked by man
If you really want to see him I think you can.
Look at the flower that blooms in the spring or the leaves turning
colors in the fall
Look at the smile of the new born child so wonderfully delicate and
small
Or look at the rain falling out of the clouds
While the lightning flashes bright and the thunder rumbles so loud.
Listen to the thunder; it is his voice that you hear
Listen to the cry of the child you hold so near.
Listen to the silence that gives us our rest
And listen to the sound of your heart as it beats inside your chest.
He is in everything you see and you hear.
God is in everything both far and near.
His voice can be loud or it may be a whisper so faint
It can be heard by any man who will listen, he need not be a saint.
God is talking to you now, I wonder have you heard?
His voice is so beautiful like the song of a bird.
Listen and my friend I promise this to you
If you follow his voice you will be gently guided through
Each lonely night you may face and any troublesome day.
The voice of God will lead you along the way.

I was inspired to write the next poem because sometimes the tongue is a
double edge sword. What we say to others can hurt or it can give them

peace. You have the ability to use your words to build a person up or tear him down. Which would you like to do?

The Power of Words

Have you never noticed the sadness in someone's eyes?
Or the look of bliss and/or wondrous surprise
Over a statement which you spontaneously have said
Your words can bring great joy or the deepest of dread
To someone who truly loves you most of all
And those words can cause them to slip and fall
Into a melancholy mood that is unhappy and filled with dread.
Or they can lift one up to float with the Angels in Heaven instead.
Have you never been hurt by the words of another?
Something said by a loved one like your sister or brother?
If his words can sting you when he says them to you
Do you not think your words can leave scars on him too?
True Love is generous and kind and good
When guided by love your words make it understood
They provoke love in return and drive sadness away
This is why we should search our hearts for the right things to say.
Don't yell out in anger or return hurt for pain.
If your brother speaks in anger love God and refrain
From words of revenge that can only return
To more words of hatred and more hurt that can burn
They burn your heart and your soul and make you forget all the love
That Jesus died for when he hung on the cross above.
Beneath him were the crowds who yelled angry thoughts and curses.
Instead you should dwell on Gods psalms and his versus.
Be happy my friend and chose your words well
For anger is what feeds the fires that have created Hell

Love is the answer to all that we do
So speak out with love and may God bless you.

The following does not rhyme but I just wanted to explain something I have
learned about my favorite of all bibles versus.

The Lord is my Shepherd!

The Lord is my shepherd, I shall not want.

Before King David was ever a king he was a shepherd. He wrote
this psalm because he knew what a shepherd had to do to keep his
flock fed.

He maketh me to lie down in green pastures.

The shepherd leads the sheep where the grass is good and edible.

He leadeth me beside the still waters.

The waters are still so the sheep will not be swept away while
drinking. They are truly in need of someone to lead them where it
is safe for they know not how to find those places themselves.

He restoreth my soul.

The shepherd looks after the sheep. If one becomes sick it is he
who will nurse them it to health.

He leadeth me in the ways of righteousness for his namesake.

Sheep are by nature, rather stupid. They can find themselves wondering off the path only to get lost and if nobody is there to help them they will die in the wilderness.
The Shepherd is there to guide them out of the wilderness to those green pastures once more.

Yea, though I walk in the valley of the shadow of death, I will fear no evil
For thou art with me.

The sheep will learn quickly to trust the shepherd, who will save them from would-be attackers or their own temptation to eat poison's food.

Thy rod and thy staff, they comfort me.

The shepherd uses the rod as a tool to prod the sheep in the right direction when they would otherwise wonder off and get lost. It also steadies the shepherd and gives him a tool to fight off any foe to the sheep.

Surely goodness and mercy shall follow me all the days of my life.

The shepherd walks behind the sheep prodding them when they wonder off and keeping them safe as they travel the trail.

And I will dwell in the house of the Lord forever.

At the end of the trail is life everlasting. A place where there is
nothing but green pastures. Nothing but still waters and nothing
but eternal beauty.

I am among all men, most richly blessed:
That, my friend, explains itself.

The truly interesting thing is we are like the sheep. We need the
shepherd. We need someone who can see where we are heading with our
lives before we destroy ourselves. We need to trust him and we need to
respond humbly to the staff which prods us to correct our ways.

Just one touch of his hands can heal your every sore.
Enter into his Fold and live in peace ever more.
Salvation is a gift from the father and the son
Understanding his forgiveness is the first step to a race well run.
Say to our Lord, I give you my all.

Carry the heavy burden no more because you heard him call.
He is the truth, the light and the word.
Read of his love but more importantly, live it each day.
I will lead you, he says. I will show you the way.
So be you not doubtful or troubled by whatever life brings to you.
This too will pass, he says. I will see you through.

JESUS CHRIST
My Lord and My Savior!

I believe I was in the ninth grade when I did a book report on the book, "Animal Farm," by George Orwell. The book was a fantasy about farmyard animals who wanted equality. This is a battle we still fight today. Equality means no matter what our religion, race or national background we are all Americans and entitled to be treated fairly.

The book Animal Farm was written about the plight of so many who do not receive the fair treatment that we all are entitled to. The next poem sums up what I understood from the book:

They Stood and Watched

They stood outside the farmhouse, looking through the dusty window pane.
Their eyes were focused on what was going inside but their hopes were all in vain.
They could see the farmer and the pigs as they talked inside the house.
They had worked for total equality from the horse to the tiny mouse.
These were not the pigs who had led the way to freedom for each and every one.
They were the great-great grandchildren now forgetting all the good that was done.
The other animals could not hear for the meeting was held behind a closed door.
"It is a ba-ad state affair," said the sheep "They care for us no more."
"I truly thought they would keep equality alive but Naay, this is not true."
This came from the horse that stood outside and watch with nothing else to do.
Said the lamb, "It's a world gone mad and it's everyone for himself it seems."

"It seems the leaders have to soon forgotten all our wondrous dreams.

"Why do we stand here and mooan," said the cow to the rest."

She said, "We should make our voices heard and tell them what we think is what is best.

Tell them all animals are created equal just as our forefathers taught.

If we forget this important fact our lives are lived in fault.

Let's tell the pigs and the farmer, too that we still believe in democracy.

Let them know if they give us less they are guilty of great hypocrisy.

There are many who say war is a necessary evil. Well I agree it is evil. However, I believe in Jesus Christ and every word he taught. The Ten Commandments were meant to be kept. One of them is thou shall not kill. I pray for our young men who have been asked to serve. I pray for their safety and I pray for their souls. One day we will live where love reigns and wars are not needed.

Rockets & Bombs

They seem to come like the rain from the hot summer sky.

People in their path will be injured and many will die.

The rockets do not know the people they will harm

For they have not eyes to see or ears to hear the sirens call to alarm.

The rockets and bombs are not guilty of any of these wrongs.

With the men who sent the bombs is where the guilt belongs.

Jesus told us to watch so we recognize this time

When nation rises against nation without reason or rhyme.

He said to look up when you see all these things come to pass.

He told us we would cry for peace and cry for peace but alas

There would be no peace until he comes to us again.

Only then will the wars and rumors of wars come to an end.

Pray to the Lord every day and all day long.

Pray for his deliverance and that it is to him that you belong.

God will end the hatred and the unyielding pain

When the time is right we will hear the Angels voices sing with no restrain.

They will sing of his love and of eternal life.

Our faith is our hope which helps us endure this strife.

Look up my friend. You will see him in his glory, coming from on high.

His love is a promise upon which you can truly rely.

I think I have already told you that there have been times in my life that I felt like God had left me totally alone. I thought he had, but now I know he was there. Without him, I would have never made it this far. The next poem is another reflection upon the love that has endured all things with me. Any strength I may have had to get through those tough times was not my own. It was a gift from God to me and I will praise him for it.

He Said, "I Am Here."

As I look back upon my life I remember times of sadness.

Sometimes, I think there were more of them than there were times of gladness.

One day I asked the Heavenly Father to answer a question that crossed my mind

I asked, "Dear Lord when in pain and sadness I searched for you but I could not find."

I asked him, "Father why did you not come to my side when I needed
you most?"

He answered my question softly through his son and the Holy Ghost.

He said, "My child. I was standing by your side and holding you in my
arm.

I protected you with my eternal love, keeping you from spiritual harm.

You may not have seen me on those sad days

But I was giving you strength in many ways.

I promised I would never leave you and a promise is never broken

I communicated with your soul although not a word was ever spoken.

So never question whether I am with you during times when you're
depressed.

I will be by your side so let not your heart ever be distressed.

I am," he exclaimed to me. "I am always with you, my son.

Through the Holy Spirit I stand beside you until your life on earth is
done.

Then look up, my son, look up for your redemption draweth Nye.

You will see Jesus Christ coming through the clouds that paint the
bright blue sky.

I am sure you all know what the expression, "as the crow flies,"
means. It means a straight line from here to the destination. Jesus said the
way to eternal life was narrow but he never said it was straight. That is why
we need that shepherd. He is the one who will prod us and guide us if we will
only follow.

When we do not follow, we will go astray. His love and forgiveness is
our Salvation. The following poem was one I wrote to give vent to the
frustration of being so human and the great joy of knowing God's
forgiveness through Jesus Christ.

It Does Not Go Straight

Narrow the way to eternal life said our Lord and Master
And narrow the way he meant.
However he also told us that we could not follow him
We could not yet go where he went.
Although he has explained all of this to us, many have misunderstood
Although the road is narrow it turns like the rivers that flow.
Narrow the road but it turns and twists
So his advice is to live right and go slow.
Look for the turns so you will not miss one and find you alone and lost.
For if we follow not his instructions our eternal life can be the cost.
Know that God will make changes for our good
Whenever he sees the need to do so
Because only by turning us around sometimes
Can we feel better about where we have stood.
So be ye not fooled by the long narrow way
For narrow does not mean go straight.
There will be hills to climb and valleys some days
As we go traveling toward our eternal fate.
So follow the Shepherd and be hopeful, always trusting in his love
For his staff will guide you around every turn until you rest with him
up above.

Let's talk about those childhood memories again. I remember as a little boy lying in the grass and watching the beautiful cloud flow overhead. Sometimes they looked close enough to touch and other times they were miles up in the blue. Come to think of it, I still like to admire their beauty, especially in the summer and fall.

I See the Clouds and Wonder

I lay quietly upon the grass, my hands behind my head.
I gaze up at the beautiful sky as the sun sets and it turns red.
My eyes traverse from the sunset to the white clouds floating up above.
They are floating in the tranquility of the mist of the blue skies love.
I watch them as they lazily move slowly with the wind
And wonder if the day will come when the clouds come to an end.
My mind can pick out shapes and forms that remind me of many
things
But most of all they look like clouds, like birds but with no wings.
They paint upon the bright blue sky I realize what it is I see.
What they really and truly look like is the breath of God to me.
So, my friend I invite you to try this little exercise.
Take some time and simply lay back and gaze upon the skies.
God lives there. God lives here among you and also me
He is the sky, he is the mountains and he is the sea.
If you have not yet found him, search him out
Then you will truly know what life is all about.

In a world where love seems sometimes to have no place to live and it is easier to hate and criticize our brothers and sisters we sometimes find ourselves wondering what this life is all about. My doctor will tell you that sometimes laughter is best medicine. If you want a medical explanation, laughter lowers the blood pressure, increases the heart rate and improves blood flow to every part of the body, including the brain. Sometimes I truly believe my brain is lacking in that department.

I like the idea of being able to laugh at myself. I like the idea of making other people laugh. I truly believe we need to exercise in being more concerned with the ability to love and learn how to keep our anger under control.

That does not mean pretend it isn't there. It means learn to love and the anger will have no place to grow. The next poem is written upon memories of my childhood.

Laughter is the Best Medicine

One of my mother's favorite things to say
Was, "for crying out loud," used when things did not go her way.
I want to change that and say with grin
"Oh, for laughing out loud" exchange a frown for a grin.
If things seem to be bleak and you lack any control over strife
Remember that God is in charge of your soul and your life
If you but ask him to come in and accept his love
You will never fear the woes of this world, you will relish in his love.
So remember that laughing is good for body and soul and spirit.
Learn to recognize humor whenever you hear it.
Or maybe it will come without a word or a sound
If you look for it in any situation, you'll find it's around.
Laugh, oh yes, laugh with all of your power
For your laughter can brighten even the darkest hour.
Laugh at me or laugh at yourself, too.
That laughter will help you live happier and longer if you do.
Now practice with me your heartiest laughter
And you will give your heart a boost for ever after.

Alright, we have talked about the beauty of the clouds. What do we think, though when they darken and cover the sun? We think it is going to be a dreary day. We liken rain as something that always happens at funeral so we find ourselves comparing it to death. In reality, it is a real source of life. I wrote this next poem as an exercise in seeing what we too often fail to see.

Gray Skies

The sky is gray this morning as clouds cover up the sun.
But, it is only morning; the sky may be bright before the day is done.
But as I survey the gray morning haze I allow myself to contemplate.
For the gray clouds remind us of dark times, something with which we
all can associate.
I ask myself as I find my mind floating in the gray skies
Are they really and truly signs of darkness, sadness and depression?
Or sent from to us to give a break from the hot suns' almighty
oppression?
Even now, as I watch the gray clouds that slowly dissipate.
It looks like we will see the sun today, although it did come late.
The sunshine makes the flowers grow but the same sun can also burn.
The very plants that depend on it from the mighty oak to the smallest
fern
For you see too much sunshine can cause them to wither and die.
That is why our Master placed the clouds high up there in the sky.
Everything here has its place and each adds to Gods' creation.
The secret is, come rain or shine, all things in moderation.
So I know as I look upon the clouds which now slowly brake away

They bring the shade; they bring the rain, with which comes a brand new day.

Oh, dear me. What did I ever do to deserve this? Dear Lord, will you not deliver me? These are just a few of the exclamations that escape from our lips during times of trial or even simply if one thing becomes a source of perplexity to us. In reality, what have we to complain about?

God has given us life. There will be disappointment. There will be some pain, discomfort and even some heartbreak. If we look past all that, we also will find blessings. The love of our family and the love of our creator should not be overlooked.

Let us all exercise in this love. When things go wrong let us look at it as an opportunity to grow in strength.

Woe is me...For Fun!

There is an exercise that I have often wanted to work at.
It's called feeling sorry for me; pity me or some such thing as like that.
The only problem is that I find I have not the time to give
For you see, this exercise affects the way I live.
It burns up all my energy and gives me little joy.
It makes me feel downhearted and easy to annoy.
I could groan about my aches and pains and cry out in the night
But what would it accomplish? It would give no me insight.
So rather than to waste my time feeling so ignored
I will throw my troubles upon the broad and strong shoulders of my Lord.
He says, "I know your every pain for, you see, I feel them too.
I hurt for you and I work for you. Your faith will see you through

I'll help you deal with each pain and each heartbreak that you may
have to endure.
For, my son I am with you now and always, of that you can be sure."
So, I think I will not waste my time on an exercise in woe.
I will look at life as a wondrous thing leading to the next life, the one I
long for so.
And where he is I will also be he promised this to me.
Where my soul will surely fly up high for he will have set me free.

This is not a poem but a story. It tells about how our eyes can be
blinded to the wonders around us. It also explains how opening our eyes and
looking for life's beauty can deliver us from many heartbreaks. Mike is a
figment of my imagination but in reality he is probably something I have
seen within myself.

A Twenty-first Century Parable

Mike walked along staring at the pavement in front of him.
His expression was that of someone walking through gloom.
Above his head was a beautiful blue sky with the most exquisite
white fluffy clouds in all sizes and shapes but Mike was not
looking.

Mike had just lost his love, or thought he had. They had
parted with unkind words and those words rang through his ears

even as he walked, drowning out the sweet sound of the singing birds and the whisper of the soft cool breeze.

Mike did not even notice that those wonderful fluffy clouds were standing right between him and the sun so, although it was a bright beautiful day the suns glare was not present, only it's wonderful light.

As Mike walked further he noticed some children playing basketball in the street using a waste basket and an old soccer ball. They ran after the ball shot for the basket but if they made one the ball would simply knock the basket over and roll out again. This didn't bother the kids. They counted it a basket and added the points to their score.

Mike stopped and watched. He became aware that they did not mind the fact that the basket kept falling over and the ball never seemed to really go in or that if it did it would simply roll out again as the basket tipped over. He couldn't help but ask one of the boys why they didn't mind.

"We don't have a real basket," replied the boy. "We just use what we have. My Dad always told me to make the best of what you have and you will never be unhappy."

Mike contemplated this but right now he did not have his love so he found little to make the best of. Then the thought crossed his mind. If the basket tips, it's still a hit. The boys still score a point. They were not expecting perfection; they were accepting things as they were. Now his mind wondered back to his love. Had he expected too much? So what if she did say things that hurt. He did that too. So what if everyday did not bring sunshine? Is there no place for rain?

It was then that Mike decided that if he could be more forgiving with his love, she might be more forgiving of him. He would make the first step. He headed home to make a call

Later that afternoon Mike was walking outside again. He had called his love. Before he could apologize she did. It seems they both knew that they were expecting too much from one another.

Now Mike noticed those beautiful clouds. He admired the glorious blue sky and he even dared to look at the sun which was just showing at the edge of one of the white clouds. Life is like that. It rains. It shines. It has valleys and it has mountains to climb. Love will overcome any obstacle that might stand in your way. Pray to God for eyes to see but once he gives them to you, use them.

The next poem can be considered as an appendix to the story about Mike.

God's Forgiveness

Our heavenly Fathers love for you and me will go a long, long way.

He guides us when we follow him and forgives us if we stray.

If we get lost on life's long highway he'll reach out to guide us back.

He wants us to know that his glorious love is something we do not lack.

Come to me, abide in me for I can give you rest.

I'll love you and I'll care for you for I know what is best.

These are the words he'll call to us to bring us home once more

He works to bring us through this life leading us to heavens door.

But if we simply turn away and follow our own dark path

We run the risk that one sad day instead of love we'll feel his wrath.

So do not tempt the Lord Thy God. Do not turn from his love

The penalty for sin is death but the righteous shall be lifted above.

He'll lift us past the sky and beyond the planets to a wonderful land of
joy

Where there is no pain and there is no anger and nothing to annoy.

Call out to your Lord and God in Jesus' holy name and then

You will be lifted up safely held in his strong arms again.

I was raised in a small church where they preached great salvation for those who are saved. I never questioned it as a child but what I did question was whether I was one of those 'saved' people. I never quite felt it.

Each Sunday evening when the minister preached I felt like the worst of sinners but I was just a child. Then, he called us to the alter. I went forward and got up feeling that I had been saved. Somewhere along the line I realized that I was getting saved again every week for I was a sinner. Did I keep backsliding?

It wasn't until I grown up that I realized that I could not save myself. God was going to have to help me. His love and grace is what I wanted most. I still make mistakes. I still get angry at loved ones. He still forgives. Jesus

said he who endures until the end, the same shall be saved. I am not at the
end yet. I guess my salvation is yet to come.

Saved!

I followed all of your commandments, Dear Lord
Now save me!
I heeded you and made plowshares out of my sword
Now save me!
I have studied your word and learned to live your way
Now save me!
I have witnessed for you relentlessly day after day
Now save me!
Why is it, dear Lord that you make me feel lost and alone?
Please, save me!
I have never been one to cast the first stone
Please save me!
You are silent when I ask for your wonderful love
I need to know you have saved me.
The silence is looming from heaven above
Please save me!
Maybe I am not going at this right
Please save me!
I feel like a fool who is lost in the night
Please save me!
Suddenly I know why my anguish is so deep
Have you not saved me?
I am but one of your many lost sheep
Please save me!
Wait, I have learned something today

You are saving me!

Suddenly I know salvation cannot possibly be earned

You are saving me!

Salvation will come to me only after I've learned

That your love for me will always be

And though I cannot earn it, I can now plainly see

That you will save me!

When the final trumpet has sounded and you lift me up high

You will have saved me!

For Jesus taught he who endures until end

It is he who will cry out you have saved me!

So for the rest of my days I will go where you send

For now I know you are saving me!

How can I possibly put into words the wonderful feeling of knowing that God is working every day with me, for me and building me to become more like the Angels? He has a tough job because I am certainly not one yet. However, with God all things are possible and I take great comfort in that.

He's here!

I dare live each day, month and year

Because I can rest assured he's here.

When things seem dark and I'm filled with despair

I take comfort in knowing that he is here.

I live life to its' fullest because I dare.

I dare because I feel his presence, I know he's here.

He is in the moon, the sun and the clouds up in the sky.

He is there but I know he is also here.

He hovers above both you and me watching from up high

I know he is there but I know he is here.

How do I know this? You may ask of me.

I answer, "For he has given me eyes to see.

The bright blue sky and dark peaceful night

I have seen his creation, I have witnessed his might.

He is the very air I breathe and all I hold dear

That is why I know he is here.

Praise him I say and praise him with all your heart and spirit.

His voice calls to you, listen and hear it.

He knows no boundaries, he knows no end

He is here. He is the sun, the rain and the wind.

He's here!

Consider the wind. You can't see it but you certainly can feel it and you could not live without it. The wind shows itself as it moves clouds overhead or causes trees to dance as it caresses their limbs. Sometimes it is angry. Hurricane winds cause great catastrophic damage. I prefer to think of the soft summer breeze or the first hint of warmth as an April breeze blows across my hair.

Winds

The wind is something fascinating to me.
It can be a whisper singing softly above a tree
Or it could be a roaring and forceful power.
It can change is moods from friendly to vengeful within the course an hour.
Sometimes it captivates us as we listen to it sing
And we watch the birds as they freely and happily wing
High above the trees and high above the ground
But other times we are taken back by the unkindly sound
Of the forceful wind which blows things to and fro
It can blow in destructive circles or it can simply go
From east to west and north to south with great velocity
Sometimes it can simply be unnoticed, laying in sweet simplicity.
Though we can't see it, it makes itself known
In summer it cools us, in winter it chills us to the bone.
When the wind blows greatly and rains fall from the sky
As lightning and thunder call out to you and I
We run to take shelter upon the approach of a storm
The wind and the rain, the clouds take the form
Of a part of nature which we cannot control
For that is indeed not a part of mans role.
Trust God!

Oh to be a kid again. How many times have we thought that? Actually as I grow older I find that I simply do not want to go back. There is too much ahead to look forward too. I am a father and a grandfather and I like it.

Yesterday, Today and Tomorrow

Yesterday I was just a child at play.

I lived in the joys of fantasy day after day.

But yesterday was limited to a very short childhood.

Sometimes I wish I would go back if only I could.

However it is now today, looking forward to tomorrow

Will it bring joy or will it spread much sorrow.

Who can say what tomorrow will bring

So I thank God for yesterday and today I will sing

Praises to he who gives life sublime.

He has control over all things, even old father time.

Yesterday has given me wonderful memories so sweet

I will treasure them and as for today I will meet

Every challenge with the best that I can give

I will let tomorrow come tomorrow for it is today that I live.

I could not change yesterday so I will not dwell on things that might have been.

I will live today as if life were beginning again.

Tomorrow will come and with it I know

That today will have become another yesterday, it will soon leave to go

And thus become one more memory for me

Tomorrow will be today and then I will see

What tomorrow holds in store but right I won't dwell
On its hopes or its fears be it Heaven or Hell!
God will be there just as he is here today
So I will cling to his love which I know was here yesterday.

There are times when we think we are facing life alone. I know that was how I felt when I had my heart bypass. As a reminder that I was not alone I found myself reciting that 23rd. Psalms that I wrote about. "The Lord is my shepherd." I reminded myself that I was not alone. The Master was in the operating room guiding the hands of the surgeon.

When I Feel All Alone!

Some days are just simply like that, you know?
There are people all around wherever you go
But in the mist of the hustling crowd you still feel sad and you still feel lost
As if you had no friend, drowning in a sea where you have been tossed
To and fro with no way of knowing which direction to travel toward
You even feel that you have been deserted by your Lord.
But you know that's not so for he is always with you
No matter where you go or whatever you do.
He hurts for you and he hurts for me
But he will not intervene until we can see
That we truly need to call and ask for his power
To guide us through each dark lonely hour.
One thing which does give me hope when I need it
Is the fact that God is always there although he is sometimes quiet.
That quiet is also there for a reason, you see.
God speaks to us but he also takes time listens to you and to me.
If he were never quiet, if we never felt lost
We would never reach for him and then we truly would be tossed.

Tossed to and fro by a world filled with anger and woe.

We would not appreciate the place, he has prepared for us to go

After we have lived this life and we are ready to move on

Heading to Heaven to which our lost loved ones have gone.

There I pray that we will live forever glad

That God helped me through the good times and the bad.

He loves you and he loves me

Oh how wonderful Heaven will be.

Yes, some days you feel alone. The secret is realizing that life was meant to be a test. It was meant to make us grow spiritually strong and this only comes by exercising the spirit. It is an exercise in faith. God will not let us be tried for more than we can bear. He will let us go as far as we can. This is how we become spiritually strong.

Life is Not a Full Time High

If you believe in God it does not mean you'll never be sad.

It does not give you reason to believe nothing will ever seem bad.

Faith does not promise that you will never be blue

You cannot always be on that wonderful high not matter what you do.

Sometimes it will seem like nothing will ever work right

But, if you believe you will know that God knows of your plight.

Life has its mountains which we must work to ascend

It also has valleys that sometimes seem to never, ever end.

The secret to all of this is so simple we often overlook.

To see what I mean, simply watch as a brook

Finds its way through the woods from where it began

To a place where it finds the ocean, so majestic and grand,

When the brook reaches the ocean it joins with the sea.

It is very much like what heaven will be

If we overcome the tragedies we endure in this life.
If we do not let our faith be destroyed by worries and strife
We will reach our home on those heavenly shores where we will be.
We'll hear music more beautiful than that of the sea.
We will sing along for the spirit will be high
In a home prepared for us somewhere above and beyond the sky
So, my friend when you find that you feel down and out
Let your spirit and soul give out a mighty shout
For guidance from God who watches over us all
Cry out to him and he will hear your call.

Ups & Downs

Some days you're up and some days you're down.
Some days bring smiles and others bring a frown.
There is one thing upon which you can be sure of.
God loves us all, he watches over you through his son with his love.
When those days come that seem to depress.
There is a wonderful exercise to help relieve stress.
That exercise my friend is a thing we call prayer.
It works because we are communicating one will care
About our joys, our fears, as well as our thrills and depressions
He'll listen if we pray and he will relieve our obsessions.
He is always there, twenty-four and seven.
He will guide us through the darkness and lead us to Heaven.
When the light shines bright he will rejoice with us all
However, we can rest assured; he will lift us up when we fall.
We will fall, my friend, we will at times feel low, sad and blue
But God stands beside us for he loves me and he loves you.
Always remember if you start out one day

And you find that it's raining or the sky is dark and gray
Those who are patient, strong and keep their faith true
Will soon see the bright sunshine that will give warmth anew.
Remember that darkness is sent to us as a time of rest
Then when you see the light you will fresh and able to pass any test
Be it sunshine or rain, be it sickness or pain
Eternal life is a gift for it he who will ordain
That you should know him, and through Jesus you see
A doorway through which you may enter eternity.

I have to admit I do have a bad habit. At least a couple of years ago it was considered to be a bad habit. I like my morning coffee. Now they have decided a morning cup of coffee is actually good for you. Coffee has anti-oxidant vitamins. They are good for the heart. Now I enjoy my coffee with a clear conscience. Actually I didn't fight with that before.

A Prayer and a Cup of Coffee

The alarm sings out at seven bringing me out of my sleep
It draws me out of my slumber so comfortable and deep.
I open my eyes and stretch my limbs as I say
Thank you, my Lord for another wonderful day.
I dress, wash up, brush my teeth and comb my hair.
I speak to my Master as into the mirror I stare.
Then I go downstairs, turn on the TV
To see what this day's weather will be.
I pour myself a cup of coffee hot and straight
It helps to bring out of my slumber some state.

Each day, Lord, I start just as the day before.
By your grace I hope tomorrow brings me one more.
The coffee will soon give my energy a boost up
But I thank you for each day as I sip from the cup.
They say the need for coffee is simply a habit for me
And I will not argue for it's easy to see
That I have started my days in the same way for years.
Like coffee, prayer is a habit but one that God hears.
He is stronger than coffee and more gentle, it's true
For with each prayer I utter, my faith he will renew.
So, I will drink my coffee and I will continue to pray
And I will continue to thank God for each glorious day.

Dear friend, do you walk in the shadow of the Lord? It is wonderful. He shades us from the burning sun of sin and doubt. He died on the cross for our salvation and he speaks to us today through the Holy Spirit. This is a wonderful source of comfort.

His Shadow

I live in the shadow of Jesus, my Lord.
Because I live in that shadow, I know where my riches are stored.
They are safely protected from the melting heat of the suns fire.
He was there to protect me since before my life had begun.
He spreads out his robe to keep me from the hot fires of Hell
His love rules my mind; yes I am under his spell.
And I wish not to ever come out of this glorious state
For it will surely lead me from this life to a heavenly fate.
His voice softly instructs me in the ways that are wise.
He has taught me that evil and hatred are what I should despise.

"Be angry and sin not," he has instructed me clearly.

For my child you know that I will always love you dearly.

So lay all your hurts, sins and your doubts upon Jesus, Gods son

And you will even see death as a doorway to a new life which will have begun.

When I was a kid we would go to the ocean every summer. I live on the east coast and there was nothing more beautiful than the glow of the sun as it peaked over the edge of the Atlantic to say good morning. The dark sky became bright and we responded by hitting the boardwalk.

These are some of those memories I cling too. But tomorrow the sun will peak over the mountain ridge and that is beautiful, too.

Watching the Sunrise

From where I live you never really see the early morning sun rising in the air.

You see it a little later once it lifts up above the mountains and peeks at you from there.

You will not see it's orange and yellows that are so beautiful to contemplate

You see a sun that is white and warm and to harsh to watch in my home state.

But, I have seen the same sun as it rises over the sea.

It paints the air and colors the water as its rays bounce across to greet me.

The sky around the sun is orange and the colors of the ocean deep and wide

Are renewed as something beautiful as the sun glances at us from the side.
But later as the sun raises up higher in the skies
I dare not look directly at it for it can blind my eyes.
God is like that, you know, he gives a moment of praise
As we gaze upon his glory as we start each of our days.
But, much of what we see we see with blind and honest faith sublime.
For those precious moments when we see him will not last a very long time.
If only we could understand that we can see him everywhere
He is in the land and sea and he is in the tree, yes he is even there.
This may come as a surprise to you but if you want a glimpse of God
Simply look inside your heart, God is there deep down inside.
He created man to be in his own image this is a fact that's true.
So we should know that a part of God is there, within me and you.
Don't walk away from eternal life for it is the one true treasure.
It is the source of a greater joy than man can ever measure.

My Dad used to say, "Don't hate. It takes too much energy." I think he was right. Hatred for any reason probably hurts the one who is angry or who allows himself or herself to hate or be angry than it does the object of those negative feelings. Love everyone. It is better for you and it is happier, too.

Isn't Hate Awful?

Jesus summed up the Ten Commandments in two great and equal parts
"Love the Lord Thy God with thy soul and also with all thy heart.
And love thy neighbor as you love yourself," he said.
We too many times forget these words and choose to hate instead.
We find it easy to hate another because of the color of his skin

We find that we can look down upon a man who does not share in our
religion.

What we often fail to see and What Jesus wants us to learn

Is that we are all works in progress Salvation is not ours to earn.

We simply accept his gift of life and we'll find he has planted a seed

That will replace all resentment and hatred with true love to meet our
need.

Hate will stand there in out way, a high impassible wall.

So high we will not see his love for the wall will grow too tall.

The happy point to make about this horrible hateful spell

Is that it is easily drowned with water from Jesus Christ's eternal well.

It means we can fill the void of hate with loves eternal glow.

He plants the seed he only asks you and I to work the soil until that
love will grow.

Remember that the seed was planted by our God and his great love.

Remember this and you will someday meet with him in the glorious
Heaven above.

Let's talk a little more about that feeling known as hatred. Jesus was
whipped, wore a crown of thorns and mocked. He did not hate. In fact he
cried out from the cross, "Father forgive them for they know not what they
do." That sounds like the purest kind of love to me. He paid for our sins.
That sounds like love, too.

High above the Crowd Below

He stood on the mountain high above the crowds below
Standing on the top of the hill
Telling the people of the Fathers love's warm glow
The crowd below listened to him quietly and still.
When he entered the city they waved palm branches as a way to welcome him
They applauded and cheered but their praises would grow dim
For in a short bit of time their praises became jeers
They mocked him and cursed him as his eyes brimmed with tears.
He once again was high above the crowds but nailed upon a cross
Yet, he prayed to the Father to forgive them for they knew not of their loss.
The sun refused to shine and the earth around them quaked that day
For the Son of God hung on that cross, the price for their sins to pay.
When I see the cross which is empty with my Lord not hanging there
It is a reminder he paid a horrible price to lift me out of deaths snare.
The empty cross reminds me that he defeated death for me
He paved the way for you and me to enter Heaven for eternity
Look up, my friend to the Lord Jesus Christ as you start each day
And as you start that day, my friend make sure to take time to pray
To the one who paid the high price for you and me and all of our sin.
And thereby wipe them away so our salvation he could win
Praise God and praise the son and praise the Holy Spirit
And praise the word of god and happy are those who hear it.

Some days you just can't get anything done. The older I get the more this affects me. I start out to accomplish something and get sidetracked and find myself doing things I did not start out to do while the job I truly wanted to finish is still waiting. That situation inspired the next poem.

Unfinished Business

I started out to complete a chore that I had once begun
But, alas I could not focus on the job until I saw it done.
I have visions of doing great things to make everybody see
That there was really something great and wonderful about me.
Oh, the disappointment when at last I walked away
Muttering quietly to myself, "I'll finish another day."
How often do we make great plans and follow glorious dreams
Only to be brought back down to earth feeling hopeless or so it seems.
Oh to be able to fly up high and accomplish a wonderful deed
But, in truth we simply do not have the patience or the energy we need.
If it was written in the scriptures, "faith without works is dead,"
Then surely we are not headed for eternal bliss but to agony instead.
"I wonder," I think unto myself, "if I expect too much today."
Does my Lord not know my limitations? Does he not love me anyway?
The wonder of his undying love is the thing that gives me faith to
proceed.
If I accomplish nothing more than to plant a wonderful seed
God's love and power will make it grow so the burden is not all on me.
For when my strength seems to have faded away his love will set me
free.
He will hold me up when I feel down and keep my dreams alive
As each day I live for my Lord my hopes and faith survive.
We all have unfinished business as we traverse through this life.
That's why we are still here on earth, with its joys and also strife.
"Keep the faith," he urges. "Be constantly in prayer as you live day to
day
And I will always lead you back if from the path you stray.

When I was a kid I either wanted to be a baseball player like my hero, 'Mickey Mantle' or I would be an astronaut. Life is funny, though. I became a radio announcer and eventually went into insurance. A heart attack shortened that career. Now I am just me. Come to think about it that is all I want to be.

If I could be

It I could be whatever I wanted to be
I believe I would be a King.
I could then make all the laws you see
For all men and women and they would be compelled to sing
Praises to me, the king, who rules their lives each day.
They would never dare to question me or fail to keep my orders.
They would know the penalty for not doing whatever I say.

Or

Maybe a King is not my style
I would be a movie star instead
I could act any part and after a while
I would be so well known my fame would last long after I was dead.

But

A movie star is only an actor, he does not really live
Accept in the minds of the audience, his fame is for them to give.

Perhaps

I would be an astronaut and travel past yonder stars.
I may soon see Jupiter, Saturn and maybe even Mars.

But

I bring myself down from the sky for the life I live is not bad.
If I could be whatever I wanted, I would keep the life I hold dear.
My wife calls me Honey, my kids call me Dad
My Grandkids call me Papa; this is music to my ears.

I love my wife, I love my kids and my grandkids are presents from
God.
So
I will simply say a prayer today, asking nothing from my God in
Heaven.
I will simply say thank you dear lord, you blessed me seven times
seven.

Dad always said, "one mans doom is another man's blessing." I am not sure I understood that when I was a kid but as I grow I have learned that we each play a part in the common purpose of life. We have positive and negative affects on our brothers. When I feel blessed I pray it is not at the cost of another.

One Mans Doom!

A favorite quote of mine has always been,
"One mans doom is another's salvation.
For it has not only to do with a mans need to sin
But also his ability to confess and receive God's revelation.
For tragedy exists all around us every day of our life
If we are drawn into its horrible snare
We will find ourselves overcome with such strife
That we will surely think there is nobody to care
If we live or we die, if we hurt or find that our life is sublime.
We will find ourselves caught up in the woes and despair.
However, we learn to accept the troubles of our time
By laying them on God for he is always there.
He loves us in spite of our own lack of love for one another
When tragedy strikes it is an opportunity for me
To help renew the faith and the life of a brother
So when the days seem dark and filled with strife

Look for the sunshine and remember the rain

Brings not only destruction but most times it brings life

Help your brother and when you do you will grow as you minister to
his pain

You both will be made stronger and able to cope with whatever life
may bring.

You and your brother can then proudly sing

To the creator of all, who works all things for good of those who believe

And even your heartaches his love will relieve.

One of my favorite gospel songs is called, "Known only to him." The next poem was inspired by that song. Truly, I know not what the future brings but I know who holds the future. That is enough for me.

I Know Not What!

I know not what the future will bring

Be it happiness or great heartache.

Still I will lift up my voice and sing

Praises to my savior who died for my sake

For God so loved the world, you see

That he sent his son to hang there to show us his love.

He lived and he died and he defeated death for you and for me.

This challenges me to search deep in my heart

And find a way to repay this glorious debt.

I will follow his way and try not to depart

From the pathways which God meticulously has set.

I will follow the road which leads to the Heavenly Kingdom

Only when I have reached it will I truly find rest.

My second promise to my Lord is that I will write about praise.

No lament of pain and sorrow but one of joy and zest
I'll write about the joy of the life as I live it for the rest of my days
And when I do finally arrive on those Heavenly Shores so sweet
I will be reunited with Mom and Dad and then I will meet
My Savior himself and I will praise him and rejoice
With the melodic sound of an Angels voice.

I am Irish. Actually, I've never been there. I am a born American but my ancestors were Irish so there is Irish blood in my body. I have been told that the Irish are a passionate people. Where faith and love for Jesus Christ and for his Father and my creator, I pray that passion will never fade.

Let Not your Passion Fade

There is no greater love than a man should lay down his life for others
There is no greater gift that anyone could possibly give
By doing so, Jesus Christ paved the way for us all, sisters and brothers.
Because he died at Calvary it is made possible for us to live
Not just upon this mortal earth but also for eternity.
For by hanging on the Cross he paid the price for the sins of you and me.
And if we truly love our lord for the wonderful price he paid
We will proclaim him as our Lord for in Gods' eyes our sins have been undone.
We will not let our fires of love burn out or even begin to fade.
But stand proudly and announcing to all that Jesus is Gods' Son.
We will love him with all our hearts and minds and all our souls forever.
For we know that his great love for us will never ever cease.
He went away to prepare a place for us somewhere on Heavens shore.
And if he went, he shall return and take us there to live in eternal peace.

So do not let the cares and worries of this world bring you down
Lift up your voices high my friend, sing praises that never cease.
For our God loves a cheerful heart and doesn't like a frown.
When our eyes first are laid upon the beauty of the heavenly coast
And when you and I hear the Angels sing
We will become a part of God's own Heavenly host.
And then forever after the heavens will surely ring
We will sing praises to the Lord our God and Jesus, our king.

That is truly my faith and I will cling to it. At this point in my life I can only see God through the wonder of his creations. He made the rain, snow, sunshine, every tree that grows and every flower that blooms. If you look with eyes that hunger for our Master you will see him in each of these and everything that we have on Earth.

Within a Rain Drop

The rain drop falls from the gray sky overhead.
It drops to the ground to find a place to land.
It may bounce off your window before it fills the flower bed
With life giving water so the daffodils can stand
And proudly proclaim the coming of spring.
We often think of rain as sad and dull
Without thinking of how it helps trees grow strong and tall.
All of life is enforced by each little rain drop
Without which, the growth of all would surely stop.
So the next time it rains watch it in wonder
And enjoy the flashes of lightning and the clap of the thunder.
For the rain will end but the life giving water stays.
It will help the plants grow and respond to the rays
Of the sun overhead which make the flowers reach for it there
With blossoms so beautiful that one cannot help but stare
At all of Gods creation and all he has done
The rain, the moon, the wind and the sun.
Look for something good in all that you see

For God put it all there for you and for me.

I was raised in a church where they really stressed the straight and narrow road. If you hoped to ever find heaven, you would not stray. I still think they had a point but I also believe today that it is a little more complicated. Jesus once said, 'narrow the way that leads to eternal life and few be there who find it.' I believe the way is narrow but where we all go astray sometimes is when we believe it is a straight and narrow road. I believe it has twists and turns that is why there are so few who find their way through. In reality we must trust in God to help us see the turns and follow his shining light. Hence comes this next poem.

Unexpected Turns in the Narrow Road

When I was young I had my plans, I thought I was master of my fate
But as I traversed down the narrow road my plans began to fade.
The road had turns but I went straight
Simply because that was the map I had made.
I would not change my plans, I would not retreat.
Only when I found myself lost did I begin to learn
That the best laid plans are sometimes incomplete.
I realized then as I began to discern
That while lost in the woods of life I could not defeat
The feeling of hopelessness, not knowing where to turn
Bewildered, confused and completely lost
The sun scorched my skin, a painful sunburn
The wooded way was where I was so I trudged on at any cost.
But wonder of wonders, what should I see
But the edge of the woods as the road turned back to lead me.
I have strayed from that road many times since then
But my Master always led me back to the road again.
Today, I am older and not so likely to stray

I try with more diligence to follow the way.
Where my savior has lead me and I find that I am walking
On higher ground, now and as I walk I am talking
To the one who cares the most for me
The one who will see me through to eternity.
So, my friend if you stray from that long narrow road ahead
Don't give up but keep your faith in God, instead.
Even the times when you do miss a turn
These are nothing more than the times when you have lessons to learn

It only seems right that the poem should follow the one you just read.
How many times in your life have you cried out to the Lord because you felt
that he had somehow abandoned you? We all do it from time to time.
Ironically these are usually the times that as we cry out, "Where are you
Lord," he is nearer than ever. Many times he is carrying us in his arms for
he knows we do not have the strength to carry ourselves.

A Dismal Feeling

I think back to youthful times when I felt lost and alone
I think back to a time when life seemed empty and unfulfilled.
I remember a time when my lonely soul would cry out loud and moan
For guidance from my Lord above to make the anguish be stilled.
I prayed to him and prayed to him but knew not what to pray for
I asked for wealth and peace of mind and treasures of this Earth
One day I opened up my eyes and trained them on Heavens door.
I realized then I knew not what my earthly things were worth.
He smiled and raised his arms to me, an invitation to join him there
He showed me riches I had never seen and joys I had never known.
As I gazed into his eyes I could not help but stare
For within his eyes was love complete that would never leave me alone.
For the first time in my life I realized he had been there all along
Sometimes we all forget what dismal feelings really mean.
Now I join him and I praise him in work, in poem and song
Those dismal feelings are only there because we have not seen

Although we see him not with our eyes, we see him with our heart.
And with his steadfast love guiding us we will not depart
From his love and from his care and from his words so dear.
Words of joy and words of love from one who is always near.

Have you ever taken time to count the sunsets in your life? Every evening it is there. It may be obscured by cloudy skies but it is still there. This is the truth about the sunset and about the creator of all the sunsets. There are there and he is there. We do not always see him. Actually, we have never seen him unless we see the magnificence of the sunset, the giant oak tree or any of nature's wonders. They are all created by God

Sunsets

The day is coming to its end as days do.
The sun is lying over the high mountain in the west.
It's been a long bright day with a sky of blue
The memory of the dawn fades as now the sun looks forward to its rest.
I watch it grow dim as the sky darkens all around
And I notice that the bustle of the day is replace with the sound
Of birds singing as if to proclaim the approach of night
But the sun pays no mind to the bird's lovely song.
It grows dim and becomes sleepy, slowly turning off its light.
Then the sound of the birds is replaced by the chirping of crickets all around.
The sun has now closed its eyes and now seems to sleep.
It is unaware of the night and does not know its sound.
For it is now gone beyond us behind the mountain so steep.
Now we rest as the sound of the night gives us cause
To take the time to join the sun in sleep.

Now for the night we put our lives on pause.
Tomorrow the sun will again arise once more.
Will it bring a bright blue sky or will rain come along?
Will there be beautiful white clouds or will they gray as the rains pour?
Either way, we are grateful for each day that comes.
Be it sunshine or rain, be it cloudy or bright.
We look beyond the sky and we can see the light.
He is Jesus!

What one of us can say that we never had one of those days when Murphy's Law prevails?

You know what I mean, there are days when whatever I try to do turns into disaster. I find myself proclaiming, "I should have never got out of bed today." That is what inspired the next write.

Wrong Side of the Bed

Have you ever awakened on the wrong side of the bed?
Have you ever had a day when everything just goes wrong?
Have you thought, "Oh, My God I wish I were dead?"
Or had one of those days when life is simply a sad song?
Have you ever had a day when nothing you start
Seems worthy of finishing because you can't make it flow.
Have you ever had a day when you just don't have the heart?
To try anything worthy of finishing at all.
I am sure that you have for my friend, so have I.
I've had days when things simply seem so sad and too dull.
Those are the days when our best cure is solitude.
Spend some time alone with your Lord and change you attitude.

A prayer to master in the name of Jesus Christ, his son
Will blow away the storm clouds and the sun will shine bright
So when life simply seems to be sad with no joy and no fun.
Look up and you can see him there in the light.
Don't let the cares of this world drag you down
For your true riches are not in the world anyway.
So keep smiling always and do away with that frown
Simply look up to your Master and quietly pray.

I am sixty-one years old; soon to be sixty-two. I have a hearing aid in each ear and even so my wife raises her voice a lot. No, it's not anger. She simply knows I won't hear what she is saying if she does not raise her voice. Even at this ripe old age and though my hearing has been impaired for several years now I still can hear my Master. I hear him with my ears but more importantly, I hear him with my heart. I hope you enjoy this next poem. I loved writing it.

Can You Hear Him?

His voice is gentle like the summer breeze.
He whispers in your ear.
He is telling you to learn to love
And care for those who you hold dear.
But even more he is calling from Heaven above
And guiding you to love everyone as he has so loved you.
If you persist in ignoring him the summer breeze will change to a
howling wind.
God will get your attention, starting you down a path that's new.

If his voice needs to become as a hurricane or the rushing sounds of
waves
He will do so for if need be he will even let you know pain
If, indeed that is needed and if your soul it saves.
Don't cry out Lord where have you gone or look to him with disdain.
But rather look within yourself and find where you have erred.
God will speak in gentle tongues or shout a mighty roar
To bring you back home to him and you'll know it's because he cared.
He cared enough to give to you whatever he needed to give.
So that today, tomorrow and eternity with him you will always live.
Listen, my friend, hear his voice calling for out for you
And never forget that he is with you where ever you are or what ever
you do.

The next poem seems to follow the first. It speaks of a God who is always
there. This one thing you can count on.

He is everything!
He is cumulous clouds floating gracefully across the pale blue skies.
He is the gentle sound of falling rain.
He is in the sun, so bright you must shade your eyes.
He is the beauty of the old oak that grows by the country lane.
I hear his voice in the rippling brook or the waves that caress the
seashore.
His majesty shows in each blooming rose
He is the wind, the snow, the air we breathe and more.
He wakes us out of sleep each morn and relieves all of our woes.
He still finds time to paint the sky with its many colors at sunset.
He calls us all together to worship him wherever we may be
He is the Lake of life, the mountains and yes even the wonderful sunset.
If we take the time to look we then surely will easily see
The wonder of our maker who reigns for eternity.

Have you ever taken the time to consider the leaf from that old oak
tree? Does it not make your heart pause between beats when you see the
daffodils bloom in May or the rose bush which grows and creates those

wonderful flowers the simply capture the sentiment of love and devotion. All of life is to be celebrated. Let's celebrate.

Consider the Leaf

The scientist will tell you the leaf of the tree
Has what they call a biological engine that allows it to be.
It collects the sunshine and evaporation from its surface
Will help cool the plant, that's part of its purpose.
The leaf collects carbon dioxide from the air around
Through the roots of the plant which draws water from the ground.
When the leaf first starts to form on the branch of a tree
It begins to grow in the form of a bud but will soon be
The source of the raw materials that nature provides
It is by Gods wondrous works by which nature abides
And the leaf on the tree is just one more way
That God gives us life to sustain us each day.
So when you look at a leaf, appreciate God above.
For the leaf sustains life, one more act of his love.

Now I have to share this. This poem is more fact than fiction. In fact it is entirely fact. We had a Dogwood tree with beautiful pink flowers that bloomed ever spring. It was one of the reasons my wife and I fell in love with our house. In the fall we watched the leaves grow from green to the most beautiful ruby red. A several years ago it got sick and died. We cut it down and left the stump. About two years later we were pleasantly surprised to see the Dogwood had not given up. It's not a tree now. It is more of a bush. But it is a wonderful thought that the tree which has long been considered a tribute to wounds endured by our Lord came back to us just as Christ rose from the dead.

The Rebirth of a Dogwood

In the middle of the yard reaching toward the sky
Stood a dogwood tree which had pink blossoms in spring.
It was sad when we found ourselves watching it die
It shriveled and found the breeze could not make it sing.
All we could do was cut the tree down.
This left nothing of the dogwood except a stump
Which we cut strait across just above the ground
And my wife placed a potted plant on it as if it were a token
Of its beauty in the spring and even more beauty when fall came around.
It was like a salute to a friend who had been lost and broken.
One day, my friend we had to remove the flower pot
For the dogwood began to reach once more for the sun
Its many branches filled in the same spot
Working toward rebirth and its battle is done
And it once again has leaves that are full and green.
As fall comes along they will turn ruby red
The most beautiful color you have ever seen.
It is reborn. It did not remain dead.
It has been given a new life, a new growth, a new start.
Just like the new life of which you have read
In the word of God which quickens the heart
And gives us the faith to live our life each day
Knowing that our Master will show us the way.
Like the dogwood we will be reborn!

I am a cloud watcher. I can get lost gazing at the many sizes and shapes of the clouds. Some are high in the sky others seem to hang low enough that you feel you could almost reach up and touch them. They are a mixture of white, gray and various shades in between. Some of them are a sure sign of rain. Others are nothing more than a whisk across the sky. The remind you of artwork drawn by the hand of God.

It's a Beautiful Day

It is a beautiful day; the sky is blue with one lone cloud floating high above.
It reminds me of cotton candy, soft and sweet and easy to love.
The sun is just rising over the mountains in the east
Its warmth alerts the trees who reach for their feast.
They stretch out their limbs as if embracing the day.
Their limbs are like stretched out arms, willing to stay
And reach for the light of the Earths nearest star.
If the trees know the source of their existence on Earth
Then we also should know of our Masters worth.
Reach out your limbs and try to touch him now.
If you cannot reach him, he will surely show you how.
Pray when you awake each day and thank God for the flower
Thank him for each second he gives, nay, each minute and hour.
Or go a little further and thank God for each day, month or year.
Thank him for a lifetime, a treasure to hold dear.
Say thank-you Lord. He will hear.

Some people live in the past. They want nothing to change. "We've always done it this way," the will say. Other people live only for today without considering the implications our actions have. The power to change our tomorrows for better or worse but they simply do not consider the dangers or the blessings in store tomorrow because of something the do today.

Then there are others who live for tomorrow. They want something better and their dreams are only what their future may hold for them.

Each of these people has found a way to go astray. We cannot dwell on things behind us. Many times the best thing we can do for ourselves is put them behind us. Those who live simply for today have a touch of truth but the question is 'are they considering what kind of world they are leaving for their children and theirs?'

Then there is the one who lives for tomorrow. He is blind to the wonderful beauty of today. Each minute of our lives should be treasured.

Three Boxes

My Lord brought to me three boxes and sat them before me.
One box was old, tattered and faded and another was hard to see.
The one in the middle captured my eye for it was beautifully wrapped like a gift.
So, I asked him why he had put them there and as I spoke the first box began to lift.
As it floated before my eyes, my Lord explained it to me this way.
He said, "The faded box that has captured your eye represents yesterday.
It is faded and lost some of its luster because it now just a memory
And as time goes on" he pointed out it will fade even more for it was only temporary."
Even as he spoke the box lowered itself and another lifted way up high.
"This," he said softly, "Represents tomorrow you know not what it will bring or why.
The box simply vanished and the box I saw next was the one that was wrapped in Gold.
Somehow I knew what he would say even before I was told.
"This is today," he said. "I have wrapped it because it is my gift to you.
Yesterday is over; its memory already grows old
But today is yours use it wisely. Show love in all you say and do.
I reflected over this for quite a while and finally began to know
Yesterday is gone, tomorrow is promised to no one
Today is a gift from our Heavenly Father and Jesus Christ, his only Son.
Pray always!

What does it profit a man if he gains all the riches of the world but does not understand the true value of life? His silver and gold cannot go with him when God calls his spirit home. He runs an awful risk of not wanting to go on for his treasures are earthly ones. Jesus said, "Lay up your treasures in Heaven."

What is a Man profited?

There once lived a man who was rich with silver and gold
But he wanted more from Jesus, our Lord
And Jesus said the man could follow him if first, his riches were sold.
The man walked away with heavy heart as if pierced by a double edged sword
Jesus told his disciples, "If you would come after me you must deny yourself"
He told them if they would save their lives they must first be willing to lose it.
For he asked that if a man shall gain the whole world and its wealth
And lose his soul what, then is he profited?
Jesus went on to ask, "What shall a man give in exchange for his soul, his spiritual health?
Jesus told his followers that they would one day be rewarded, each according to his works and some
Would not savor the taste of death he said
Until they saw the Son of man in his kingdom.
They saw him arise after three days from the dead
As they did; believe in him and you will find true freedom.
Trust in him and follow him and let not your hearts be troubled, my friend
For when they hung our Lord upon that cross that was not the end.
HE LIVES!

He Sends the Rain

He sends the rain, he sends the sunshine

He makes the warm breeze blow.
He creates the lightning's jagged line
And makes the thunder come and go.
He sends us summer to warm our souls
Autumn is a glorious gift of his love.
He even made the sweet song created by a dove.
He never stops amazing us with all his wondrous creation.
We plant the seed but he makes it grow out the earth's cru station.
His voice can be mighty like the thunder
Or gentle as a soft summer breeze.
He is the great creator of every wonder.
He never rests he even makes the cold winter day, causing lakes to freeze.
If you look for him, you can see him in everything, everywhere
So everyday when you awake, thank him for being there.
He is!

I was raised in a church where they stressed, "Do good for others and thereby receive stars in your crown." They believed this was the way to earn your way into Heaven. I disagree. My entrance into heaven will be a wonderful gift. If I do good deeds it nothing more than my way of saying "Thank-you Lord."

Why do Good Deeds?

Is our road to Heaven paved by the good deeds we do?
Is eternal life a reward from God for accomplishments here on Earth?
Have I earned my place in Heaven for helping you?
Or have some special place reserved with special worth
Because I have paid my ties and given money to the poor?
Have I somehow earned God's love with these deeds?
These are all questions we need to ask, for sure.
The answers are surprising; we do give to those in need
But not to earn a special place in God's Kingdom.
This we must accept as a gift freely given.
Only then can our deeds bring spiritual freedom
Or the right to sit with our Maker in heaven.
Because we love him we will help our friends
Because he loves us he will lead us along
To follow the path that never ends

Until we find ourselves in the Kingdom of God
Not because we earned it for this we cannot do.
The deeds do not come from us or earn as much as a nod
From our Heavenly Father for these are his tasks which we pursue.
First comes Salvation and then the works really mean
That we have met God and our soul has truly seen
The need to follow where ever he leads
Salvation is born but comes in this order, you see.
First, he is the one who plants the seeds
This brings about the works that lead to eternity.

A Warm Summer Night

I lay in bed on the verge of sleep one night
A warm summer breeze flowing through the window.
Just as I was ready to doze off there came a flash of light
And the sky gave out a mighty rumble of thunder.
Then in the mist of this I heard the pitter of raindrops upon the glass.
They quickly spread across the ground asunder
Bringing life to the grass which was brown as brass.
I crawled out of my bed and watched the rain fall
At first it was soft but soon came in sheets driven by the wind.
It was now not pitter patting but pounding on my window and outside
the wall
Again the lightning lit up the sky with flashes and streaks of majestic
light.
Now I could feel the raindrops upon my face for the wind was driving
it inside and out.
I didn't bother to close the window though the rain was falling on
everything in sight.
I had been praying for rain and now it was here, an answer from God I
have no doubt.
There was music from the trees and the flowers, the grass and the
ground
As if praising God for the rain, what a wondrous sound.

They say into each life a little rain must fall
This is true and if it did not what would happen to us all?

That Was an Angel

I dreamed that I was walking down a road in the dark of night
When a car came speeding down the road toward me.
I had no time to step aside; it was only then that I saw the light.
I thought to myself, no way out do I see
And the light must be the essence of God.
For the car would surely strike me down
But what happened next was wonderfully odd.
I embraced my Lord for he lifted me up from the ground
And I expected to keep going toward Heavens shores.
Instead, I was returned to the road below after car had passed by.
"Why did you not take me?" I asked. "I was ready to enter through
Heavens doors.
"I am not your Master," said the one from the light.
I am one of his Angels who watch over his sheep.
I keep them safe from sins danger and might
And too watch over them always, even as they sleep.
If it had been your time to go, I would have lifted you to Heaven above
But the Master still has things for you to say and do.
He is asking that you spread his compassion and love.
God promises every thing you give will be returned unto you.
Love ye one another!

Caution, They Are Breakable

Be careful how you treat them for they are breakable, indeed.
If left in tact they will assure you of a life that knows no sorrow.
Unfortunately, this is only a dream for we all break them in times of
greed
We all get caught up in a desire to assure life's comforts, today and
tomorrow.
We break them when we do not take time to help one who is in need.
We have all fallen short of perfection and have not followed after the
Master
We have all broken God's law. We have often strayed from his holy
word.
If we break even one of the Ten Commandments we leave ourselves
open to disaster.
However, our sins are all washed clean by the wondrous grace of the
Lord

If we but admit they are there, he will calmly make them disappear.
Jesus made it easy for us when he summed the commandments up
Love the Lord with all thy heart and soul and thy entire mind and
cherish his love so dear.
And love thy neighbor as thyself. That means share with him from
your cup.
We will try and we will fail but with God's love his rebuke is waved.
Through the life, death and resurrection of Jesus Christ you and I will
be saved.

It's been a while since Hurricane Katrina bashed New Orleans and parts of Mississippi but the damage in many of those areas have not been repaired yet at the time I sit and write this. I wrote the following to bring attention to the devastation these storms can cause.

Katrina, Oh Katrina

You came storming into town amidst great confusion and fear.
You blew apart the homes that these people held so dear.
Your winds had no mercy as they called upon the waves
To wreak havoc upon the city as the lightning streaks and the thunder
raves.
You showed no heart and took no pity on the people whose lives you
took that day.
You even sent the rain from up above as you blew their homes away.
But the human heart does not give up and with faith they will rebuild
anew.
So, blow all day and blow all night and send your rain and waves too.
Because when you are but a memory man will start again
To rebuild all that he held dear before your wind and rain.
It is written that the rain falls on the just and the unjust too.
This is a fact that I have seen before and I know it's true.
But even the heartaches that life may bring rain, fire, drought or the
waves
Only serve to bring us closer to god, that's how our soul he saves.

Laughter, the Best Medicine

You've heard it said, I'm sure
That if you laugh the world laughs with you
But you cry alone for they will ignore.
They know not what pain may make you cry
And may not even ask what they might do or say,
To ease your pain and rid your tears for they know not even why
You shed those tears, so naturally, they can't make go away.
This means, my friend, it is up to you
To be the one to brighten up your world today.
I know exactly what you can do
To bring tears of laughter to your eyes.
Find some humor in anything
The benefits will bring a wonderful surprise.
You will soon find joy and your laughter will sing
It is good for your health, any doctor will tell you
And more importantly, you will find happiness within.
With each burst of laughter your lungs are cleared like new
And your spirits will surely rise again.
So laugh hard and long and keep a smile on your face.
A frown turns people away but they are welcomed by a grin.
They will see your smile which will serve to erase
Their own problems and give them a new frame of mind
My smile is your smile and yours is another's
And we all share our smiles like sisters and brothers.

The Big Storm

It came slowly out of the Caribbean Sea.
It seemed to grow in density.
Everyone was braced for the devastation it would bring.
Another hurricane has now taken wing.
Everyone on the coast was fearful wind and rain it sends.
They tied down everything to protect from its winds.
But then the storm became gentler as it moved on.
The might of the hurricane was never born.
As the storm reached land it simply brought much needed rain fall.
There was a collective sigh of relief which was shared by all.
Ernesto turned out to be a much needed gift
From God in Heaven, so join me and lift
Up your voices unto God for his wondrous love.
He sent liquid sunshine which falls from above
And replenishes the soil and waters our lawn.
Praise him for our payers are answered and the rain has fallen.

Fly, Like a Bird

I gaze into the clear blue sky
And watch the birds as they gracefully fly.
I try to imagine how it would be
To fly up high ore land and sea.
From up there I would feel much closer to heaven's door.
I could spread my wings and gently sore
Through the clouds and sometimes above them.
With wings outstretched I would reach for God while praising him.
One wonderful day my spirit will take wing and fly
To meet face to face with my creator who reigns on high.
I will bough my head before my Lord,
Quietly praising him without a word.
My mouth will be still but my spirit will sing
Praises to the one who has given everything
That I might have eternal life.
No more will I need to deal with cares and strife
But instead live where joy and happiness can abound.
The glorious voices of Angels singing is the only sound
That my ears can hear and my heart can beat too.
For Jesus died on the Cross for me and for you.
Praise him!

Not What It Seems

It has been raining for the past two days
And the rain is still pouring from the sky.
A light wind blows raindrops, causing sprays.
As I looked out my back window something caught my eye.
There is a lone flower in a giant flower pot sitting in the rain.
It is sadly drooping its head as if it did not dare to look at the sky
However, as I watch it bending low as if in horrible pain
I am made aware that there is no pain for the flower is soaking the cool
raindrops
The weight of the raindrops cause it to relax and bend its head low
The flower patiently awaits the return of sunshine once the rain stops
But for now, it simply accepts the needed rain and wind that will softly
blow.
My friend, do you not see that God's plan is even written in the rain?

The rain will nourish the plants and the sun will call to them.
With glorious rays of light creating once more its bright refrains.
Then the flower along with the birds and the trees
Will reach out to the sunshine's warmth and light
Life is renewed for each of these
The flowers stand up tall and birds take to flight.
New life has come to all things on earth
Just as we will experience with our own rebirth.
It is all a part of God's holy decree.
A new life for you and new life for me.

When I was twelve years old I was taken to the river and baptized in the name of the Father, the Son and the Holy Ghost. The baptism is a symbol of Christ's death and resurrection. It is the symbol of our rebirth spiritually.

Because He was Baptized
So Are We!

It was a glorious day when Jesus visited John.
It was on that day that Jesus came to him and said,
"Baptize me," for he knew this was a sign
Showing that man's sins can be forgiven and their lives made pure
instead."
John forbad him, saying, "You should baptize me."
And Jesus answered, "Suffer it to be so for it is meant to be."
So john baptized the Lord, with great passion and love.
Jesus rose straightway out of the water and lo,
The Spirit of God descended upon him like a dove.
As it lighted upon him, they all heard his fathers' voice

Saying, "This is my beloved son, in whom I am well pleased,
John baptized with water but the Holy Ghost will cleanse you to make
you rejoice."
Jesus then explained, "You will be baptized by the Holy Ghost giving
power and joy
as your burdens are eased.
Your hearts will be made free of sin causing you to be bear witness of
the Fathers love
To all that you see of the Father wondrous love, for it was meant to
be."
He also explained to them that he is the anointed one,
Saying, "All power on Earth and in Heaven is given to me.
Go and teach all nations, baptizing them in the name of the Father and
the name of the son.

John baptized Jesus. Later he came into Jerusalem as they waved
palm branches and heralded him as the King of Kings. The celebration did
not last long for they did not understand why he came. That is why the next
week he would be crucified. He paid the price for our sings.

There He Hung

How ironic it was that this should come to be.
He was hung high above the crowds hanging upon a tree.
It seems only fitting that he should be raised up high.
He came from above to the Earth where he would die.
He came to Earth to pay for sins of you and I.
He came to Earth to show us the way.
It was a high price for our sins that he came to pay
And he hung without anger but with love he did say
Father forgive them, for they know not what they do.
He held no anger or resentment aimed at me or at you.
He knew the cost that would be paid was for our salvation.
He realized that without his love we would live in desecration.
"Why then?" you may ask. "Did he come from Heaven above?"

He came for he realized that we all needed his love.
We could not pull ourselves from hate, sin and resentment.
Without his wonderful love we would never know contentment.
We would never learn the art of meeting our neighbor with a smile.
We would not know forgiveness for forgiving was not our style.
He walked on the Earth that we might all learn
To love one another and let our spiritual lights burn.
As our Lord hung there high on that cross
He did not condemn us but delivered us from a great loss.
A loss of our spirit and a loss of our soul were bought back by God's
Son.
And his very last words while hung on the cross
Was Father, forgive them for they know not what they've done.
Can we pray that prayer? Can we show that love?
If we can, we are promised a place in Heaven above.

I have always said my two favorite times of the year are spring and autumn. I say that in spite of the fact that I have allergies and the pollen count is extremely high in both spring and fall. For that matter, it's high in summer, too. I like the mild warm but not hot temperatures. In the spring I love to watch the Dogwood, cherry trees and flowers bloom. In the fall I revel in the wonderful kaleidoscope of colors as the trees turn an array of colors.

Signs of autumn

Trees dancing in a brisk breeze,
Leaves scurrying across the ground.
Their colors range from green to yellow and from gold to brown,
As more of them disengage from the trees to fall to the land.
The nights get cooler, as do the days.
The clouds seem to rise higher in the sky where they form bands.
Autumn's beauty can be appreciated in so many ways.
You can sit on a park bench and watch the leaves fall
Or walk through the woods and hear the birds call.
You lose yourself in the flying clouds up high
Or watch as the geese fly south as they take to the sky.
It's a colorful time and there is so much to see
One must take time to admire the work as the tree
Prepares itself for the oncoming winter with its rain, wind and snow.

It is all part of our creators plan as we watch seasons come and go.
From spring to summer, to fall and to winter,
It is exciting for us as each one we enter.
Enjoy, and Praise God!

He Sends Them All

He sends the sun, he sends the rain
He sends us all four seasons
He gives us courage to endure any pain
And gives love to forgive for many reasons.
He sends us blue skies and skies of gray.
He even made the clouds that float above.
He does let us hurt some days
But it is all part of his love.
The sun warms us the rain gives life
And the pain we endure brings us stronger hearts.
Those blue skies envelope us, protecting from strife
And the clouds entertain us as they build and part.
Again I tell you this all part of his love
For he wants us to wax strong
So one day we will be with him,
Once ascending to Heaven above.

In whom the god of this world hath blinded the minds of them which believe
not, lest the light of the glorious gospel of Christ, who is the image of God,
should shine unto them.
II Corinthians Chapter 4, verse 4

I Believe!

I believe for every drop of rain that falls
A flower grows.
This sounds like the beginning of a hymn that calls
On anyone who can honestly say he or she knows
The savior and through him the father of us all.
Yes, the raindrops fall upon the seed and then it grows.
This is how he saves our souls and makes us his.
He lifts us up when we fall down and heals our woes.
If you do not know him or of his love you will surely miss
The wonderful chance to become one of his and have a happy heart.
Don't turn away, my friend for he calls to you

"Come to me and never depart.
For my love will guide and watch over you, too
I will heal your pains and make you sing
Rejoicing in my love and light
I will heal you from all of sins vial sting
And give you peace of mind, as well as inner strength and might.
So you can stand up to the deceiver and never let him win.
And even when you fall, my forgiveness will give you sight
And draw you home to me again."
Trust in God's love and live in delight.

A lot of people are asking the question, "What would Jesus do?" In the world we live in today would he take a different stand than he did more than two thousand years ago? I think not. One thing our Lord told us all while still with us is that if you do good to others this is doing the will of God. There is a lot of talk about morality these days but somehow the morality everyone wants to talk about is limited to a few items. Love is a matter of morality, feeding the poor is a matter of morality. Educating our children and teaching them right from wrong is a matter of morality. Jesus once told a parable where the master proclaimed, "I was hungry and you fed me not." He proceeded to say, "As you have not done it unto the least of one of these you have not done it to me." These are all a part of morality.
Pray for guidance and he will lead.

Are You a Laborer?

Are you a True laborer of God above?
Would you give of yourself anything you can?
Can you meet even strangers with a smile of love?
Would you befriend your neighbor, be it woman or man?
Would you give up some Earthly comforts to help the poor?

Would you pray for the forgiveness of one who has hurt you?
If you can honestly say yes to these it will not bring you to Heavens
door
But it is a beginning so please do not these things neglect to do
So do not hesitate to give of yourself and your love.
Do not look down upon your neighbor or the poor.
When you have prayed for the forgiveness of others to God above.
Add more to this list, as you build on them you find yourself at
Heavens door.
When the door swings open you will be invited in
Not because you did the works but because you loved the Lord.
For each good work will wipe away a sin.
And when you are ready, you will know the word.
I forgive and I also give unto you the gift of eternal life
I will cut Satan down with the power of my sword
And deliver you from all of life's care and strife.

Therefore said he unto them, "The harvest truly is great, but the
laborers are few: pray ye therefore the Lord of the harvest, that he
would send forth laborers unto his harvest.

Living Rage

Do you know what our biggest problem is today?
Rage, it takes on all forms and sizes and shades.
There's road rage, experienced when someone is in our way.
There is the rage of a parent over the mistakes their child made.
There is a special kind of rage aimed at the family next door
Because they don't mow their lawn or prune their flowers any more.
We feel that anything which is not just as we like it
Is a personal affront to us but we will not admit

That sometimes we need to understand that life does not revolve
Completely around us so if we should want to resolve
These conflicts that we fight with day in and day out
We must show more compassion and be less likely to pout.
Things will not always, in fact some times rarely will, go our way
So we must learn to take a forgiving attitude and practice each day
The art of showing patience, forgiveness, encouragement and love.
All are gifts to us sent from or Master in Heaven above.
They were sent to us not that we should hold on to them
But rather we should love our neighbor and always encourage him.
Only when we have mastered this impossible chore
Will we be ready to walk up and knock, then enter Heaven's door.

Childhood Poems

Remember those poems we used to chant
When we were only children?
Now, I try to remember them but try as I may I can't.
Some of them are best forgotten for they were really crude.
The fact of the matter is that some of them were simply downright
rude.
But we sang them or recited them so many times in our youth
That now we may even find our minds replaying and that's the truth.
Of course there are the high school cheers we used at football a game.

But, I'm afraid that some of them now make me hang my head in shame.
I wonder what Jesus meant when he said, "except ye be as children."
I must admit some of my days of youth I remember with chagrin.
I suppose this is one more example of the forgiveness of our Lord.
Children are children and always will be and that seems like the final word.
However, as I look back I am made to realize that we were not perfect in every sense
But we were still growing and learning and that is our defense.
My point here is that God knows our hearts and he also knows we grow.
A child will grow and learn about things of which he does not know.
So when Jesus said except ye be as children, what he meant was this.
Keep growing and learning and expand yourself and always be one of his.

About the Size of God

Look out your window on a clear autumn night.
Now scan the blackness for those specs of light.
Admire them, consider how big they are.

Allow yourself the see each tiny star.
Consider it as a sun much like our own.
Try to understand that it is not alone.
It has friends which pepper the clear autumn sky
It is amazing that they can be seen by human eye.
However, we see them as tiny lights.
We cannot see their true brilliance and powerful might.
Miles and miles of space stand between us and them.
Now hold your breath and let your mind swim
Through the void of space and consider this.
God is in all and created all with nothing amiss.
He created our sun; he created the stars and the moon
And he created Heaven, "Lord I am coming soon!"
How big do you think this creator could be?
He is all and in all that you and I can see.
He is even bigger than that, he is in the mystery of universe.
Yet, he has called on someone as small as me through every verse
Of God's holy word and through the voice of Jesus, his only Son.
He will bring us home when our earthly chores are done.

If I Could Be:

If God said I could be anything I wanted to be.
I know my response would be, "let's see."
If I could be anything I wanted to be I would surely ask to simply be
me.
Why me you may ask? If I were a bird I could fly free
And glide high over land and over the sea.
Maybe, I could ask to be a man as rich as can be
But I tell you I would still rather be me.
You press on telling me I could be an owl in a tree
Not knowing the dangers of the world around me
But the owl knows of these dangers you see
That is why he never blinks and he stays in the tree.

"Why do you not wish to be a king and people would bough before thee?
You ask and you ask but my answer is one of simplicity.
What I really want to be is what God made me to be.
I am his handiwork for I am what he made me.
Should I then say, "God I implore of thee
Please make me something you had not wished me to be?
I tell you my friend just as those birds fly over the sea
I will one day fly higher held in his arms for eternity.
God made you and he also made me
He will give eternal life, forever in ecstasy.

When Demons Come to Visit

They come in all sizes and shapes, you know.
They are not always goblins or ghosts.
They can be subtle with profiles low.
They can breed within your very own mind, dwelling on the things that you fear the most.
Sometimes they come as your very own thought, telling you, "this I cannot do."
They will cause you to give up your dreams and back away.
The depression overwhelms and makes your mind stew.
It dwells in anger and disappointments of the day.
But you have within you the power to overcome the lack of hope.
Simply search your heart and soul and you will find.

A source of faith that never lets you fall and attached to this strong
lengthy rope
Is the master of us all who will help mold your mind to believe you can
fulfill your dreams
You need only the faith given by God to try.
For if you believe in God and Jesus Christ, it's never as hopeless as it
seems.
Simply never look down and set your goals high
If you insist on pushing forward, he will be there to give you the power.
This will help you fulfill your greatest dreams.
You will thank him for all your successes because he lifted you out of
your weakest hour.

The Misery of Unsaid Words

He loved her with all his heart.
He would have given his life for her rather than let her know pain.
He knew his life would be empty if one day they should part.
He had already promised that always by her side he would remain.
The only flaw in this wonderful romance was the words he
never said.
He had given earthly gifts and earthly comforts instead.
The words, "I love you," did not come easily through his lips.
Even when he felt her hairs caress his finger tips.
He always took for granted that she knew just how he felt.
One day God called her home, now he felt his heart burn and melt.

She always knew how he loved her; she never needed for him to say.
Now it was he who wished he had said it on this cold September day.
It is an exercise in passion, love and warm emotion to softly proclaim
your love.
They are words you will keep with you until you, too are lifted above.
Tell your loved one of your passion; do not wait for a reason.
It need not be an anniversary or a special time of season.
Say I love you. Go now and do it today.
Then watch what happens, and you'll see that's not hard to say!

Psalm 24

1 A Psalm of David.

The earth *is* the LORD'S, and the fullness thereof; the world, and they that dwell therein.

2 For he hath founded it upon the seas, and established it upon the floods.

3 Who shall ascend into the hill of the LORD? or who shall stand in his holy place?

4 He that hath clean hands, and a pure heart; who hath not lifted up his soul unto vanity, nor sworn deceitfully.

5 He shall receive the blessing from the LORD, and righteousness from the God of his salvation.[1]

This is a Heavy Load
(Can you carry it?)

The Earth is the LORDS and everything that dwell therein.
That includes you and I, be we pure or guilty of sin.
Be vigilant, my brother for if we sin we smite the Lord.
We do this and thereby place ourselves above the word.
The word, you see is Jesus Christ who died for us all.
He lovingly and obediently heard his Fathers call.
He came to Earth to pay the heavy price for our transgressions.
He came for our forgiveness and listens to our confessions.
We have all fallen short of the Glory of God.

---

[1]Excerpted from *the Complete Multimedia Bible based on the King James Version.* Copyright (c) 1994 Compton's New Media, Inc.

It is for that reason that Jesus came to Earth and he died
High upon a cross he hung for all of our sakes.
He endured the pain as they mercilessly drove in the stakes.
When he arose, he showed to Thomas his scarred hands and feet.
He promised us he had paid the price for us; the price for our deceit.
Let us all turn to him for spiritual strength to love
Love our neighbor as ourselves and most of all, our Father who is
above.
Father, I am coming soon!

The Healing Power of Rain

Life can seem dark, dismal and bleak
It can seem that everything brings on more pain.
At times like this you strive and seek
For healing but find only more hurt to your distain.
When you are feeling helpless and weak
Talk to God as you watch the rain.
Through Jesus Christ, he delivers us all
From all our heartaches and relieves our soul.
For just as the raindrops wash off the soil
They are like the Holy Spirit for its goal
Is to wash away our cares and help us toil
To perform the will of Our Heavenly Master.

It can bring good even in the wake of disaster.
When life hits you with horror and you have nowhere else to turn.
Trust in God and believe on his son
Never stop praying until life on earth is done.
Call on God and you soon will learn
That his everlasting love goes far beyond the sun.
He is calling to you and to me and guiding our every turn.
Let us serve him throughout this earthly life and do not fear to live
Be the best that you can be each and every day.
Do all you can and give all you can give.
If you fail, he will forgive and cast your sins away.

It was a blistery cold day in March with those winds you expect in this month of the year. I watched from inside where the glass shielded me from the frigid cold of the blustery March wind. I couldn't help but notice how it made the trees sway too and fro as if they were awakening and preparing for the April showers that were soon to come and the warm summer ahead. I was reminded that the March winds were not so different from the autumn when the trees were readying themselves for a long winters nap. That is what moved me to write the following poem.

The Trees are dancing!

Outside my window nature puts on an extravagant show.
The trees in the wind are dancing, waving to and fro.
As the wind caresses their leaves they move in unison.
They seem not to miss the absence of the sun.
Today is gray; the rain has now finished its fall.
However, the wind is still leading the dance to the left and the right
Insuring the perfect choreography of trees, grass and all.
An occasional leaf blows free from a tree here and there.
They are an added attraction of the September ball.
As I watch them float quickly across the lawn I simply stare.
The beauty of autumn is taking control

I feel the temperature dropping as the wind takes on a chill.
The song of the wind and the dancing of the trees touch my soul
I have seen many autumns but it moves my soul still.
For soon the leaves will put on a glorious show
The colors will blend together, painted by God's hand.
As the next few weeks pass I will watch as one by one they go.
The leaves leave the trees to rest in peace. All winter it will stand.
Unadorned and uncovered except by an occasional snow.
The trees patiently wait for spring when their leaves and blossoms
return once more.
And then they will start their cycle all over again, a life renewed.
I have watched this wonderful cycle many times before
I have savored the spring breeze, summer sky and the autumn I
reviewed.
Yet, somehow I never tire of the sight.
Let us enjoy beauty of the autumn day as well as the spring night.
They are all gifts from God.

He Was

He was a young man who had been taught to believe.
He has accepted Jesus Christ as his savior, whom he did adore.
Upon finishing high school he felt compelled to leave.
Saying good bye to his loved ones he joined the Army to fight in the
war.
His Mom and his Dad and his beloved Ann prayed for his safe return.
Then he came back from the horror which he had now known.

He soon realized that to love Jesus Christ he would soon have to learn.
He would have to overcome the seeds that war had sewn.
He would have to pray and search deep into his own soul now.
What he would find there, he was afraid to know.
But in the violent wave the war had changed him somehow.
Now his mind seemed to follow where ever the wind would blow.
He had been thoroughly trained in the ways of war.
Now he had found that he knew not himself anymore.
He prayed with the help of his loved ones each day.
Through prayer they helped him once more find his way.
He accepted Jesus Christ again and then followed his lead.
Love overcame the horror and hatred giving peace to one in need.
Others had not the courage to face what they had become.
They gave way to lives of violence, causing the death of some.
And others found themselves in prisons behind the wall
It was the ways of this world that caused them to fall
However, we can't allow criminals to run free.
So prison is where those war heroes's must be.
It is sad but true, they learned to kill for God, country and to survive.
Now there is little peace where their souls will arrive.

Let us pray for them all. They are our son's and daughters.

Gloom begets Gloom, Happiness Creates Sunshine

Have you ever noticed the power of your own mind?

If you dwell on disappointment it is trouble you find.
If you spend your time bemoaning life's horrible tragedies
You do nothing more than cast away all positive strategies.
If you dwell on every disappointment as if it left no hope
You find no reason to strive for happiness no matter how you grope.
Let's take a few minutes and think on what's good and bright.
Let us admire the blue sky or a cool autumn night.
Let us not be put down by life's disappointments and troubles.
Dwell on the problem without considering a cure and the problem doubles.
So, let us stand up and cheer for no definite reason
Remember, God gave us a life to live, no matter the season.
There is something to praise him for every day of the year.
We have loved ones to care for and those we hold dear.
Look for the good in everything that you see
And good will is the salvation of you and of me.

The Dream

Last night I had a wonderful dream in which I was flying high.
My body and spirit were one with each other as I traversed the clear blue sky.
Just as I thought I would surely see darkness in the vacuum of outer space.
I saw two arms reach for me, a man in a white robe but I could not see his face.

I kept watching for the blackness to envelope me as I raised high above the land.

However, the darkness never came and I now focused on a hand.

It was reaching for me and a voice so sweet was beckoning me to join him.

I took hold of one hand and the second as I heard Angels singing my favorite hymn.

The music became louder and louder but I didn't mind its sound.

I rose further into his loving arms and he said, "You were lost but now you are found.

The music of the Heavenly Hosts was too beautiful to describe with words.

It was by far the most beautiful sound that I had ever heard.

I found myself crying out, "Dear Lord, please take me for I am yours."

But he answered, "My child today is not the day for you enter through Heavens doors.

I still have work that you must do and kind words that you need to say.

So return, my son and give love to all you meet on each and every day.

Bare witness to my Son Jesus Christ and teach the words he spoke.

When the time is right I will come for you and that was when I awoke.

I lay in my bed for a long time thinking of the wonderful, glorious dream.

I found myself praising god, for my soul has truly been redeemed.

Do you know something? We all want miracles. The question is the; do we recognize one when we see it? I am a heart patient. I have been through several operations to save my physical body. Heart bypass surgery takes great patients and skill. The knowledge that God gave to the doctors who are responsible through him for my being here is a miracle. No, not like Jesus who simply said go they way, your sins are forgiven but still a miracle.

What is the cost of a Miracle?

How much does a miracle cost, ten cents or ten thousand dollars?
Anyone who tries to buy a miracle, my friend is a person who simply squalors.
You cannot put a price on a true miracle, be it changing the water to wine.
It can also come through the skilled fingers of the surgeon who has saved a life like mine.
Our Heavenly Father works in mysterious ways, sometimes quietly and undetected.
However, he watches over us all to make sure our eternal life is protected.
He does not always speak through a burning bush as he brings to us his healing.
He sometimes works through our minds quietly with a thought or a subtle feeling.
He does his work so quietly because he builds our faith that way.
For if he was to prove himself through everything he did each day.
Then faith would not be necessary and we would cease to search him out.
When our searching stops, our growth stops, too and we forget what his love is about.
Therefore, my loved ones let us not ever give up the mystery of Gods love.
Let us always keep searching for a closer walk with him, thereby lifting ourselves above.
God does not judge us for constantly searching for truth as we live each day on Earth.
For when we learn something new each day we thereby compound its worth.

John, Chapter 20 Verse 29 Jesus saith unto him, Thomas, because thou hast seen me, thou hast believed: blessed *are* they that have not seen, and *yet* have believed.[2]

I have friends who keep sending me cartoon quips by that character, "Maxine." One that I thoroughly enjoyed is a picture of her standing before

---

[2]Excerpted from *The Complete Multimedia Bible based on the King James Version.* Copyright (c) 1994 Compton's NewMedia, Inc.

a mirror and exclaiming, "Getting old ain't for wimps." I can identify with that.

It is morning!

I am awakened by the sound of music which cuts short my rest.
I climb out of bed, looking out my windows at the mountains in the west.
They stand proudly there as they did yesterday and the day before.
Soon, I am heading for the shower and as I walk through the door
I see my reflection in the mirror and scrutinize how the years have taken their toll.
My hair has grown gray and my body painfully complains to my soul.
As I step into the shower I feel some relief from my pain.
I feel the water washing ore me as a warm summer rain.
Downstairs in the kitchen my coffee is brewing.
As I dry off I can feel my body and soul renewing.
Now I am ready for another day of life.
I know that the day may bring joy or great strife.
That cup of coffee I sip from helps clear my mind.
However, as is drink it my soul is searching to be realigned.
For each day, I search my spirit for renewed enlightenment.
I quietly breathe a prayer that even I do not hear
I send a message of love to the one who is always near.
"Dear Jesus, son of God," I quietly pray.
I thank you for it is now another day.
You have given me once more life renewed
My mind quietly reflects and all my yesterdays are reviewed.
However life starts again with today, and then comes tomorrow.
I know you will stand by me through triumph and sorrow.
The greatest joy about growing old, perhaps the only one
Is the joy of feeling closer and closer to God's only Son.
This is a day, the lord has made.
Let us be grateful and rejoice in it.

The Breath of autumn

Autumn has sent relief from summers overwhelming heat.
We shut the AC off and opened the windows. Then I calmly took a seat.
As I sipped from my cup of coffee I watched the curtains dancing in the autumn air.

They were happily flowing too and fro without a single care.
As the autumn breeze pushed past them through the window and
caressed my cheek
I simply allowed myself to enjoy as I stretched my neck to peek.
I looked out past the drapes through the window at the clouds of
shades of white.
They were merrily dancing in circles and ordaining the blue sky, such
a wonderful sight.
I began to play the game I had played when I was just a child.
I watched as I saw the different shapes, my eyes scanned every cloud.
While I was doing this the breeze continued to blow gently through my
hair.
I relished in the coolness of the wind as my eyes continued to stare.
Some clouds were moving in circles while others were floating high
above.
The cool gentle autumn breeze is one more proof of God's great love.

In The Early Morning

There is something special about the early morning sunrise.
It marks the beginning of a brand new day as I awaken and open my
eyes.
I look out my window at the rising sun ore the mountains in the west.

I liken it to the second coming of my Lord on the day I will gain my rest.
It is a constant reminder of a new life in which there will be no disappointment.
For my Heavenly Father sent his son some two thousand years ago.
He was dead but defeated death and will come again I know.
He said, "I go to prepare a place, then I will come again.
And if I go I will come again to lift you from earthly sin.
He said, "In my Fathers house are many rooms if not I would have told you so.
One of those rooms I will prepare for you and my Fathers love you will know.
The tempter may cause you doubt or lead you to go astray.
Do your best to not follow him and kneel before God and pray.
Pray a prayer like this and pray it from your heart.
Dear Lord I pray in Jesus name that you not let me depart
From the love of the one who hung on the cross to relieve me of my sin.
I sing praises to the one who walked once upon the Earth and soon will come again.

AMEN!

What Do we Fear Most?

DEATH looms overhead and can inundate the mind.
It leaves no peace; it allows no joy for it means we leave life behind.

It stands between us and our lives, causing loneliness and pain.
We look upon death as an evil thing for it cuts off life's refrain.
Jesus must have felt this horror as he knew it was preordained
It was only through his death and resurrection that our hope for life
was gained.
So he put his fears behind him as he humbly carried his cross.
Had he not taken that morbid trek up the hill it would have meant our
loss.
He cried out from the cross as he hung there for you and I.
He did not hang upon the cross so we would never die.
He hung there so we would shed the fear that burns deep within our
hearts.
First we learn to embrace our lord and then our reassessment starts.
He came to show us that death is not the end for it truly starts a life
that's new.
That is why he cried out from the cross, "Father, forgive them for they
know not what they do.

Yesterday is Gone!

This morning the alarm went off playing "When the Saint's Come Marching in.

That is a beautiful way to start the day as I awaken once again.

It takes just moments for me to become aware that this is a brand new day.

It is only once now and then that I consider life this way.

Yesterday is over, you see. It has been replaced by today.

Only now and then do I ask myself, did I help someone in any way?

Yes, yesterday is now a memory for it has run through its allotted hours.

What did I do to make yesterday a day to proclaim God's powers?

Did I help the poor; did I comfort the sick, or visit someone in jail?

Did I say something to help my brother in any way or did I simply fail.

God knows my every deed and he knows my every fault.

He knows when I have strayed away and when I have followed what he taught.

When I find myself pondering these things, I am reminded of this one thing.

I cannot relive all my yesterdays or go back and change anything.

However, today is now and I can make the most of this gift that God has granted me.

So if I dwell at all on yesterday, it is only to help me see.

I can see missed opportunities and this makes me more aware.

It makes me see the things I might have done and thus help me to prepare

To give back to the master in some special way the things that he will ask.

It may be a simply smile to stranger or it may be a Heavenly task.

Whatever he wants of me today, I pray I will succeed.

When today becomes yesterday I pray I will have done some good deed.

Love one another, even as your Heavenly Father has loved you.

Do not judge me my Friend!

Do not judge me, my friend for if you do so
You are judging yourself more than you know.
If our beliefs vary from one another as we live
This does not mean you and I have nothing to give.
We do have the love of our Lord and Jesus Christ, his Son.
And when we accept him our journey has only then begun.
We must dwell on things in common we share.
We should not fall into the trap where we point and stare
At a brother who does not come to Jesus in the same way
For the roads that lead him to our lord may have been through clouds
of gray.

If we cast judgment and do not attempt to understand his heart and
soul
We are the ones who have not yet reached our spiritual goal.
That is to love and to give of ourselves through his holy name.
For it was by love that to Earth our Lord Jesus Christ came.
Try, therefore to understand and be slow to criticize
For if you judge your brother this could lead to your demise.

Let your faith ring out like a bell by the way that you live
And do not cast judgment but never fail to give.
Give to your brother from your heart love that's real and pure
For one day, you shall find yourself standing at Heavens door.
And when you do, I pray you will know God's wonderful grace.
As he looks back ore your life, your footsteps, he will trace.
He will see the times you have forgiven others
He will welcome you in to meet with heavenly brothers.

Deadly Silence

When one is in love the one thing that can cut through his soul like a
knife
Deadly silence, no response and not even an angry word, the creation
of strife.
They say words spoken in anger can be deadly and destructive
And so they can be, but they can also be instructive.
However, when one simply says nothing to show that they care.
This is a deep void which can cause a loved one to despair.
"Why will you not tell me what it is I did wrong?" he may ask.
And if she gives no retort, her silence is a mask
This will not allow an exchange and no clue to a solution.
It has caused many a love to grow cold and drown in its own pollution.
For if you truly care for someone you will fight for their love.
Your passion will not allow silence; it will help you rise above.
Above the problem which you have, whatever it may be.
Otherwise, you and your loved one will feel as if lost in a raging sea.
With no hope of reaching land as dark clouds swirl above.
Break the silence and forgive one another, it's an act of great love.

Unfruitful Sleep, wondrous awakening

My sleep was not a restful one as I tossed and turn throughout the night.
I dreamed I could not find myself for I was surrounded by darkness looking for the light.
I called out to my Heavenly Father but he was nowhere to be found.
I walked alone in the pitch black darkness, unable to see and not hearing a sound.
I heard only my own voice calling out and coming back to me as an echo.
I had no idea where my foot steps led me for I could not see where I go.
"Am I walking into hell?" I thought for God seemed so far away.
Is the one place I feared most of all where my eternal soul would have to stay?
Ahead of me there shown a light but only long enough to glimpse at it.
It sparkled and then it faded away from above where I stood in the black pit.
When I had all but given up, I saw the light again.
This time it grew brighter and a voice said "I will forgive your sin."
That is when I opened my eyes while lying in my bed.
I breathed a prayer of thanksgiving to God as the morning sunrise cast its glow of yellow and red.
Dear Lord, I prayed I thank you for I have seen another day.
I thank you Lord that your love has guided me as I trek along the way.
I pray you will not leave me alone, not knowing where I go.
I pray that you will always be my comfort and teacher as I live and grow.
He whispered into my ear, "My child, "you will reap good things, if good things you sow.
In doing so you will never know the loneliness you have just dreamed about.
You will know love, compassion, and encouragement but you will have no room for doubt.

We live in a time when prayer has been taken out of school. They want to teach evolution instead of Bible teachings. If you believe in Christ but you are an American citizen this can create an awful conflict. Can we truly love both when one does not love the other? Dwell on that. I will give you a hint. The answer is yes but you must chose which one you will serve.

I Am Your Country

Help me, I beg of you. Help me for I need your insight.
Being a democracy is not easy; to keep it one must be willing to fight.
I need to know that you care about what I am and what I have become.
I will never be able to stand for long with the same beating of the drum.
Please do not ask what I can do for you, but what you can do for me.
If your interest in me fades and dies I can never keep you free.
I am not hurt if you criticize if it is something that we can mend.
There is nothing unpatriotic about looking for problems on which to tend.
What is unpatriotic is becoming complacent leaving me to believe
That you are no longer interested for it is to your heart that I cleave.
Be concerned about the character of those who would be part of your government.
Ask them to explain what they stand for before your vote is spent.
Please know that your complacency is the cruelest pain to me.
Let not your hearts grow cold or uncaring having given up all hope for me.
Only with your undying love can I remain free from sea to shining sea.
Pray to God each day that I fall not under the wait of my own corruption.
If this happens no one will remember the values that brought about my inception.
Please keep in mind, my friend that if in corruption I do fall.
My broken heart and soul will be debris covering one and all
So learn about the people who ask you to give them your trust.
Cast your vote and take your stand and do what' ere you must.
Stand tall and fear not to proclaim the things that you have believed.
If we work together the wondrous dreams of our founding fathers can be retrieved.
I am the U.S.A.

I may have already mentioned that as a child my folks would take us on trips to Skyline Drive in Virginia every autumn just as the leaves were putting on the most extravagant show ever. Such a wonderful kaleidoscope of colors. Such a breathtaking view from the overlooks high in the mountains was a thrill we looked forward to every year. I guess that is one reason I am always writing about the seasons, especially autumn.

Seasonal Changes

I was out riding today and I noticed the clouds are moving higher in the sky.
It is as if they are saying, "We need to make room" but for what I wonder why.
The sky is changing its hue. It is now a different shade of blue.
I scanned the mountains and admired the trees for they are changing, too.
Until now, the colors have been subtle, just barely enough to see.
Now the leaves are turning to red and yellow, some dropping and quietly blowing all around me.
The temperature is taking on that special chill that only comes with September.
As I admire God's handiwork, I now pause, contemplate and remember.
As children my brothers and I would rake the leaves into a single pile.
Once the pile was high enough we would dive into them for a while.
Eventually we would tire of this game and our Mother would make a demand.
Those leaves needed to bagged and burned as per her command.
Along with the chore we were told to do, we received a wonderful treat.
As the autumn breeze fanned the burning leaves we planned for something sweet.
We found some sticks and took a bag of marshmallows, a gift from mother dear.
Roasted marshmallows were a treat to enjoy, one more blessing of this time of year.
Now I have grown older but I still have memories that are sweet.
My memories include the birth of spring as well as the summer heat.
It also includes the autumn breeze which cools the earth, preparing her for rest.
After this came snowy winters with icicles and winds with rising zest.
Winter, summer, spring or fall, I know not which I love the best.

Frustration

Frustration eats away at ones resolve.
It can cause our confidence to dissolve.
Frustration brings our mind to a halt.
If creates anger and idle hours can be the result.
Frustration is a destructive force
It causes uneasy feelings from which we cannot divorce.
Frustration feeds upon itself and grows.

If we resign ourselves to it resignation grows and it shows.
How do we break this evil curse?
How can we cause the anguish to disperse?
One way is to quietly pray.
Pray for guidance throughout each day.
Ask God to stand with you through frustrations charge.
With his help you can overcome any problem, be it small or large.
So, let not your heart sink in disappointment with no hope.
If you do so, you will not have the faith you need to cope.
The world will sometimes be cruel and unforgiving.
You will find yourself asking why you even make an attempt at living.
When things go wrong and they surely will do so.
Keep your faith strong and even the hard times will help you grow.
Pray to God through Jesus Christ, he son.
You will meet them both face to face when your Earthly journey is done.

Color Me

Color me blue for that is the color of the sky above.
Color me red, like a valentine, the color of love.
Color me green, each and every shade of green.
Or if you like you can color me yellow, bright and clean.
Or simply choose a color from the colors of the rainbow.
If you like you can color me shades of white and gray like the clouds as the wind blows.
Whatever color you paint me from the outside, please do this for me.
When looking into my soul here is what I pray you see.
I pray you will see love and joy which does not lack.
For without these things my soul would turn black.
My soul would be void of the Passion of my Lord.
I would then find it easy to take up a sword.
I would cast away life as if I had no purpose or recourse
Except to inflict pain upon others without any remorse.
Color me the colors of the rainbow that arches above.
I beg you, Dear Lord to color me with love.

Apathy, the Great Destroyer

We all know guns, bombs and wars cause the great destruction of all.
We all know that hatred and violence can cause many good men to fall.
We somehow overlook another form of cancer which threatens our dear land.
The great destroyer, apathy makes our soul too weak to stand.
We take what we have for granted and we refuse to see what is bad.
We simply say, "This too will pass." We forget the dreams our forefathers had.
They wanted us be a great nation. A nation the world would admire.
Over centuries of being a nation, we have grown weaker and easy to tire.
We have also been guilty of putting ourselves on pedestals, placed on high
If things go wrong we simply hang our heads, feel sorry for ourselves and sigh.
Have we really forgotten that this land of ours was bought by the blood of others?
They fought and died for you and I, this makes us one and all to be sisters and brothers.
Leave us not become complacent to the sorrows which surround.
Let us sing for God above to hear the majestic songs that we sound.
Do not allow complacency to become our nation's norm.
For if we care we can solve our problems and our country can reform.

Dare to Dream

Dreams do not always come true, you know
But, if you do not dream your wishes simply go.
Let us look at why we fail to follow our dreams.
One reason is pessimism, or so it seems.
Pessimism will cause many a mind to stall.
If you dare not dream, you have no plan at all.
There is a word for a plan to overcome this treacherous stalemate.

Optimism can help you press on before it's too late.
If you dare to dream it may not come true, you see
However if you dare not to dream it will definitely never be.
So be courageous and dare to follow that dream.
Cling to it and work at it no matter how hopeless it may seem.
If you do not accomplish this dream, dream again.
You will learn from your failures and accept your accomplishments
with a grin.
Allow yourself to follow your heart
Keep in your mind that your dreams are a start.
Just as a man who is building a house sits making a plan
Dare to dream of accomplishments greats and believe that you can.
The true failure for us all is never allowing ourselves to try.
Hence, we find ourselves hopelessly wondering why.
"Why did I never do great works," we say.
The answer, my friend is that we let doubt get in the way.

Love
Let your heart beat freely and don't bother to count the beats.
Over time you find that knowing Jesus is the biggest of all treats.
Very often, you find yourself praying great prayers of thanksgiving.
Enjoy this wonderful feeling for with it life is worth the living.

In case you haven't noticed the first letter of every sentence above
Spells out that magical word, when you give it you receive it from those
that you love.
L is for laughter and also for letting others enter your heart.
O, is for overtures of songs of praise for the love Jesus did impart.
V, is for victory in Christ and eternal life with the Master in his
kingdom.
E, is for every good deed you do and for your eternal freedom.

Love is the answer to the most important question ever asked by man.
So give your love to anyone and everyone you can.
Jesus Did!

The Autumn Beauty

Leaves floating from the trees, dancing to and fro like snowflakes so
light.

They are not all white like the snow but colors of red, gold and yellow glimmering in flight.

The trees are putting on one final extravaganza before they sleep for the winter months.
I am reminded of trips with my father as a boy accompanying him on one of his hunts.

I watch the squirrels and rabbits as they prepare their homes for the long winter.
They instinctively know when the cold winds blow they will need a place to enter.

Have you ever traveled on a mountain range marveling at the wondrous colors from afar?
My Dad would take us on Skyline Drive and we would watch through the windows of his car.

It seems that every season has memories attached, reminding me of my loved ones who have gone before.

Though I cannot meet with them at this point in time, I will embrace them, of that I am sure.

Some people think that autumn is a time of dying but I see it as a cycle of life.
I see its beauty and I see its hope which causes my heart and soul no strife.

Take time, my friend to enjoy this season of the year
And share it with those that you hold dear.

I Count the Heartbeats

I lay my hand upon my chest and listen for the beat.
I hear first one then another and within a second it will repeat.
Thump-thump, the heartbeats come in succession.
My heart feeds my body as blood comes in progression.
Sometimes I wonder at the miracle that is my heart.
It works hard all day and all night, life to impart.
What keeps it going, why has it not quit?
It must get weary but cannot rest a bit.
Thump-thump, it beats just like a drummer.
It keeps on working come winter or summer.
I have often wondered what it will be like when its song is through.
It lies quietly while my spirit ascends into the blue.
The heart has performed a wonderful service to my soul.
Now it is resting for it has fulfilled its role.
God, I pray my heart never beats in vain.
I pray I have made something of my life that remains.
Something that will have changed the lives of others.
A heart that beats loudly in the service of sisters and brothers
If you give the comfort of this knowledge to me now
I will sing songs of praise to you eternally, this I vow.

We all love, Love songs. We sing about heartbreak and we sing about patriotism. In this day and age, we feel self-conscious about singing abut God and Jesus unless we are in church. We feel strange about praying in public. Just this week a girl was chastised for reading the Bible in a school cafeteria.
Is it any wonder people are killing others with no excuse or reason? We need to turn back to God. He is calling.

Sing to Me

As a child who lies in his mothers arm I listen for a song.
The sound of her voice is a comfortable sound for I know to her I belong.
I long to hear my Lord's voice which sings songs of joy and comfort.
I listen for his voice and can hear it in the wind if I but make the effort.

He sings a special song of love as raindrops fall around me.
His song can be heard in the rushing waves as I sat by the sea.
His voice can be soft and subtle so I must listen if I would hear.
He often speaks in a whisper, singing "I will hold you near."

However, if I am not listening I may miss the sound of his singing.
I may not even notice the wonderful sound of the church bells that are
ringing.
His voice is heard in every ring of every bell as it is in the beating of my
heart.
If I but listen I will hear the knowledge which he will gladly impart.

The secret is to use my freewill, a gift which he has given to me.
But freewill is like a double edge sword for we build what will come to be.
If we use this will to follow our own selfish desire we have swung the
sword the wrong way.
If we freely will ourselves to follow him, he will come to us that day.

And when the final trumpet blows and we are called home to stay
We will thank the Lord that he guided us along life's treacherous way.

I wrote the next poem on a whim. I am not even sure I knew where it was
leading until it leads me there. I trust in God and I watch the seasons come
and go. Maybe that is why he wanted me to write this. Whatever the season,
it is a step toward my savior.

The Cool October Breeze

It is October; it is the month of Halloween.
It is October; the trees are shedding their green.
It is October. The clouds are lifting higher in the sky.
This is the month when temperatures fall
And the breeze comes with a sigh.

We don our sweaters and jackets for the temperatures are dropping.
We prepare our fireplace and gather wood and build a fire that soon
will be crackling and popping.
It is October; as we watch all living things preparing for the climate
change.
The trees will soon have dropped their leaves; now gray replaces green
as we scan the mountain range.

It's all a part of life's constant cycle and the trees and flowers sleep
through the winter snow.
We will watch the mountain range turn from gray to white and then
back as snows come and go.
It is October and leaves are flying past my window.
I watch and I admire the winds as they cause the trees to dance to and
fro.

Soon we will see the winter snow and then the rebirth of spring.
This cycle of life seems as if it is a never ending thing.
However, all things come to an end and what becomes of us then.
I simply trust in God for I know I will live again.

Nay, I will simply move from this world to another cycle of life.
I trust he will show me where I may live without care or strife.
Think about eternal life. Is it not a prize to win?
Is it worth praying to Jesus Christ who will wash away our sin?

Look up for your redemption draweth Nye and your cares are cleared
away.
You can know the love of Jesus Christ today and every day.
It's October, and I see God's work all around me everywhere.
I know that whatever tomorrow brings he will give me strength to
bear.
So I will pray and trust and work for Jesus because he first died for
me.
So on this October day I look above the clouds and Heaven I can see.

There are those who think that science has disproved the existence of
God. I firmly believe what we have learned about the world only explains
how he performed the miracle of life. There are those who are so caught up
in this new age of electronic conveniences that they have no room for such
old fashioned ideas as prayer. I believe God has brought us here. Now he is
waiting to see how we deal with it.

Modern Inconveniences

Electronics has given us many gifts.
Medical science offers everything from healing to face-lifts.
We drive around in cars that go fast.
The horse and buggy days are a thing of the past.
Cell phones go wherever we go.

We have knowledge of things our forefathers did not know.
Television and computers give instant access to the news.
Alas, sometimes this is simply a door to the blues.
Let's look back to the days when our ancestors thrived.

It was faith from which their happiness was derived.
They were not bombarded with instant news of the events of the world
of gloom.
They were given time to deal with troubles that may or may not come
to loom.
They lived one day at a time and trusted God for tomorrow.

They enjoyed life's happiness and dealt with all of its sorrow.
Today, we have convenience they never dreamed about.
We also deal with sin, crime, sorrow and doubt.
Let us absolve ourselves from the faithless times in which we live.

We can derive much more pleasure if only we live to give.
Give to the poor, give to the sad and give to comfort those who are in
pain.
Pray for the world and for your friends and pray that your faith can
always sustain.
Let not science become the destruction of your soul and your heart.
Trust in God and know the joy that only he is can impart.

The next poem I dedicate to my wife. She works the night shift as an RN.
She lives during the day as a wife, mother and grandmother. She is love.

She is An Angel of Mercy

She is an Angel of mercy in more ways than one.
She works through the night until comes the rising sun.
She is a nurse who looks after her patients as they rest through the
night.
She answers their pages each time they turn on their light.

When she gets home she is another kind of angel, so dear.
She is a wife, mother, grandmother who loves those she holds near
We are all her loved ones for she says we make her life worth living.
She derives her joy from the love which she is giving.

I worry that she does not get enough rest sometimes.
I watch as she sings to the grandchildren and reads nursery rhymes.
She grabs a few winks of sleep throughout the day.
Tonight at eleven she is again on her way.
Angel by night and angel by day
She is my Angel for her love will not sway.

I chose not to make a rhyme out of this. I chose to simply write down my thoughts and faith. This was inspired in part by a poem submitted by Steven Curtis Lance. God is the sun, we are the moon. We never quite touch him but he touches us with his brilliant light.

Another Sunrise

Have you ever watched the sun rise in the east?
And then turned to see the moon setting in the west?
It is almost like they are soul mates who see each other
For just a moment or two with the whole world between them
And yet they are bound by a wonderful connection.
The light from the sun is what reflects off the moon
Creating the lesser light that rules the night.
So, though they are always so far away they are brother and sister.
The sun and the moon are almost always connected by light.
Only once in a while is there a night when the moon does not receive
the light from the sun. Maybe, this is what it is like when we feel cut
off from God.
I believe it is during these times that we search and that is a good thing.
Search for him when you do not feel his presence. Pray for him when
you hear only silence. Have faith to know that sometimes we let the
world stand between us and God.

If we call for him, he will always be there even when we do not feel his presence. If we search for him we will find he had never really left us but only pulled back so we would search him out. This is our salvation.

Seconds

Tick, tick, the clock is on the move. We awake each morning as the
sunrise beckons.
Days are made up of hours. The hour made of minutes and minutes a
group of seconds.
There is little time for us to look back the next second has already
passed by in a flight.
Perhaps we would not be so overwhelmed if we thought in terms of
hours or days to give us better insight.

But the truth is we live each second to get through each minute and so
on throughout our life.
We will make mistakes and clock will strike, those errors cannot be
erased.
As every second or minute passes there are obstacles that must be
faced.
Although we cannot change those instantaneous mistakes we make.

We can count on God's everlasting love which forgives us for Jesus'
sake.
Oh, but we must first admit the mistakes of which we are guilty of.
We must search through the seconds and minutes of life and then
simply trust in his almighty love.
You see it is not a hopeless thing for God is the Master of all time.
So, be reminded of his glorious love, shown through Jesus Christ each
time you hear the clock chime.

Angels are watching over you and me. They are sent by God through the
Holy Spirit and they are calling us away from sin and doubt and to eternal
life. All we need to do is follow and believe.

Have you Ever Seen and Angel?

Have you ever seen an Angel? Well, neither have I.
At least, I have not seen them with human eye.
But, somehow I know they are here because they sing.
When I am feeling low they make Heavens Chimes ring.

They touch my life in such subtle ways that I cannot explain.
All of life's heartaches cannot hush their voices as they proclaim.
They tell of God's love and Christ's sacrifice.
They tell how the Master delivers us from vice.
They sing of the wondrous view of the shores of heaven above.
They sing of undying and never ending love.

I know they are near although my eye cannot see.
I know that they work through my life. Their charge is the welfare of
me.
Not of my body for it will soon be gone but of my soul for it will live on.
When my spirit leaves my body and journey's above
I will meet them and thank them as they lift me in love.

I will fly away to join my Master and sup with his son
My Earthly adventure will have been finished and done
The next life will be for eternity with no end but everlasting glory
Only praises and songs of gladness will be heard and that is my story.
Have you ever seen an Angel? I have although not with human eye.
I have seen them with my heart and soul and they are coming in the
sky.

I wrote the next poem during an election year so we were hearing a lot
of debates about the state of our nation. Some of our leaders or would-be
leaders were arguing the facts. Do we have a strong economy? Why then,
does it cost so much for a gallon of Gas? When I was a kid, a gallon of milk
cost a quarter. Now it is nearly two dollar for the same white liquid. When I
was a kid it was possible for the local grocery store to thrive. Now they have
been driven out of business by large food chains and department stores are
now giant malls that buy their products overseas and sell them to you and
me. The question troubles me. Do we actually make anything here at home
anymore?

High Finance

Our politicians today will tell you the economy is strong.
Who among us can really tell if they are right or wrong?
However questions keep playing across this uneducated mind.
If they ever analyzed the facts I wonder what they would find.

128

The first question is a simple point of definition.
What is it that they call a strong economy? Do they mistake it for inflation?
Yes, some who are already blessed with great earthly riches say the economy is strong.
However the middle class is paying for their wonderful success so this cannot last long.

Let me tell you what I believe a strong economy would be.
There would be enough food, clothes, housing and comforts for you and also me.
And there would be more left over to help those who have no home but live in boxes under some tree.
When anyone was seen in need they'd never have to ask, for there would be people who would simply want to help them out and try to guard their health

Yes, those multi-million dollar businesses would want to share their wealth.
For their millions will serve no purpose when there is no middle class.
Without the balance of distribution of wealth, it will soon simply pass.
And when there are no more weak to trod upon, this is a fact of science

That it will simply be a matter of a battle of the giants.
Aggression begets aggression and anger brings the same.
So our strong economy is really only strong in name.
Strength means balance and balance tips the scales not at all.
When the scales are tilted our economy is doomed to fall

I am sure you are like I am. There are certain memories which will never leave you, nor do you want them to. My uncle had a farm about a half hour drive away and he invited the whole family each Thanksgivings Day to come and help with the butchering. Along with the great time everyone had, everyone got some fresh pork to take home with them. We, the kids went to see our cousins and simply enjoy each others company. That is what inspired the next poem.

Seasonal Memories

Every season has memories that it can share.
Its autumn now and I stand in the coolness of the air.
It brings back flashes of when I was a child at play.

When we would pile up the leaves and then dive in where they lay.

I remember when every Thanksgiving Day we went
To my uncle's farm, oh the happy hours we had spent.
My uncle raised hogs and on Thanksgiving Day the whole family came.
The grownups would be hard at work while we kids ran to play games.

My Aunt would cook a glorious dinner of Turkey with all the
trimmings so tasty.
Then we all enjoy it, including pumpkin pie and a variety pastry.
But, my favorite time came late in the day when the pork was brewing
in big pots in the barnyard.
Before the grownups would make up the puddin', they would crack
open a bag of salt on the table

And we would feast on the pork for as long as we were able.
Those were happy days I remember with my Mom and my Dad
Along with my Aunts and Uncles and the great times we had.
There was also the knowledge that Christmas was only a month away.
But, for now we were content to just enjoy Thanksgiving Day.

I fear some of my friends may disagree with this poem but I spent my
whole childhood trying to be saved only to find out that I could not save
myself. That is a gift. What I am trying to say is this. Jesus came to pay for
my sins. He told the woman at the well to "go and sin no more." We don't
know what happened to her then. I believe Jesus did wash away my sins.
But just as Paul wrote, "I am the greatest among all sinners," I fear so am I.
The secret is to constantly keep soul searching. See my faults and failures
and work at removing them from my life. I honestly believe that if I do that
his forgiveness keeps going. And now I think my soul is ready for another
Wash.
I'm coming Lord!

The Car Wash

My wife and I took the car to the wash and turned on the powerful
spray.
We worked together to clean off the dirt but no matter how hard we
worked some of it would simply stay.

When we turned off the water, we grabbed some wet towels and frantically began to scrub and clean.
However, no matter how hard we worked there were still spots to be seen.

We finally gave up because of sheer exhaustion and decided the car was clean enough.
But I still found myself looking at the dirt, tempted to grab another cloth with which to buff.
We finally both decided that we would live with the small amounts of debris stuck to the car because it was much cleaner than before

We agreed that we would say the job is done well enough. There was no need to do any more.
Now, I look back and realize that our lives are like our car.
Our Lord Buffs, and polishes and works for our souls but he does not wipe away every mar.
He knows the sad truth that we live in a world of sin and doubt.
So, he says, "I will wipe away the important sins and the residue will teach you what life is about.
Christians are not perfect. Christians are forgiven.

The next poem was written as a tribute to my Mom and Dad. Mom was hard working and it broke my heart when she died of Cancer at the age of 54. But I know she is with God. Dad is there with her. Dad only got as far as the sixth grade in school when my grandfather died and he quit school to work full-time to take care of Grandma. But even with a sixth grade education, he got a job as a sheet metal worker, building F-27 airplanes at Fairchild Aircraft. I still have a watch that was given to him after 25 years of service. This man could take the car apart find why it was not running right and put it back together. He and his car took us on many wonderful trips. In the fall, Skyline Drive would call to him and we would ride and look at the beautiful mountains of Virginia as they turned so many brilliant colors. Today, everybody needs a college education, they say. Dad didn't.
So, You Want Memories?

My fellow writers it is a monster that you have created today.
You have put me in the mood to let my mind go ahead and sway.
It takes me once again to my long ago childhood days.
When we had no computers, we entertained ourselves in other ways.

My Mom could be harsh but she loved us and we knew it.
My Dad had many chores to do but always found time for us a bit.
When I was very young we did not even have a TV set.
Cell phones and satellites had not been invented yet.

But those were times when we found happiness in the simplest things.
It was fun to simply play on the floor and listen to Mommy sing.
And Dad was a special person, though he didn't have much of an
education.
Still he had knowledge and he was never, ever short on dedication.

In short, I would not trade places with my children for any price you
may name.
We did not need Nintendo; we would make up our own game.
Dad would take us hunting for squirrel or maybe we would hunt
rabbit.
This we looked forward as fall came and it was a Saturday Morning
habit.

We did not eat like kings, but we didn't starve to death either.
We would hunt and sled in the winter time until the cold made us take
a breather.
Oh, those wonderful memories of when I was a youth.

But, I must admit that I would not go back and that my friend is the
truth.
Life is a glorious journey that God has planned for us each and
everyone.
So, though I will always have my memories I will live each day till it is

done

The other day as I was hurrying through the grocery store I came to the end
of the isle and almost ran into a lady who was coming from the other
direction. I excused myself and said something to the fact that they need to
make these isles wider but as I spoke I was smiling. She had been in hurry
but when she saw me smile, her face broadened into one, also. I had a
similar situation on many occasions. I have noticed that when I am smiling
the other person will most times respond in kind. Isn't that a wonderful
thing?

A Smile

Have you ever noticed the power of a smile?
It is a contagious thing and never goes out of style.

A simple smile says, "Excuse me," or it may say, "I like you."
It may say lots of things but there is one thing that is true.

It will almost always bring a smile to the face the person receiving it.
And if it radiates friendship and a certain amount of wit
It can cause a person to say hello when, otherwise they would never
speak.
It generates friendship which so many people seek.

And the funny part and also, what makes it oh so sweet
Is the fact that the other person will most likely pass it on to the next
person they meet.
So if you start the chain you never know just how many people you
have touched.
You see, my friend this is a fact that you cannot smile too much.

Your smile will reflect on the others persons' face
And they will pass it on to another who will pass on again and thus you
start the race
With a single smile and a jolly hello you have planted seeds of
friendship everywhere you go.
Where does this chain of smiles end? You will never know

But what you do know is the fact that once it starts growing.
You may touch hundreds of lives without even knowing.
Now, ask yourself. Is this not a good thing?
Does it not create as much joy as the hymns we sing?
Smile and the whole world smile with you.
It is a human relation tool that is tried and true.

Johnny Cash had a record out before he died called "Ring of Fire." In it he
sings about the tides that bind. It got me to thinking while listening to the
song the other day. What a beautiful thought, "The tides that bind." It is as
if we are all in an ocean so large and yet the tides seem to bring certain
people together. God, in his infinite wisdom knows what we need and who
we need. It is true that all things work for the good of those who love the
Lord.
The Tides that bind!

When I was newborn my mother held me in her arms.
My parents coddled and nursed me and protected me from anything
that harms.
Those are the tides that bind.

When I grew a little older I found someone to love.
It was as if she was sent to me from God above.
My love was returned and soon we too were one.
Married and expecting our first born son.
Those are the tides that bind.

Two more children were added to our life.
We loved all three through joy and through strife.
Those are the tides that bind.

Now our children are grown and found their own true loves.
They have blessed us with grandchildren, more gifts from above.
Those are the tides that bind.

Life has been an uphill journey but I have had someone to travel it
with me.
The past is just that, and the future we have yet to see
But I know that God has been watching over me.
He has sent me a wife and children to love with all my heart.
He has given me the ability for true love to impart.
Those are the tides that bind.

The most important gift he has given is the life of his son.
I will carry his love till my life on Earth is done.
For I know that all that I have are gifts from God who watches over
me.
He will guide me, nourish me and give me eyes to see
That his love is not ending and his forgiveness never fails
He protects me, strengthens me and comforts me through whatever
ails.
Those, my friend are the tides that bind.

Have you ever wondered how we got to where we are today? We
should be happy. Most of us have homes, cars, expensive clothes and we eat,
perhaps too well. All this does not bring happiness. Have you searched for
it? Have you searched in the right places?

What's Funny about Life?

Do you know what is funny about life?
People....
Do you know what causes most strife?
People....

Why is it that even the things that should give us a peaceful feeling
Will too, often cause our minds to go reeling?
Why can we never simply enjoy God's eternal love?
Why is it so that negativism is something we cannot rise above?

We often find ourselves dwelling on problems and blinded by the
beauty all around us.
We worry and stew and create all kinds of a fuss.
We see only darkness when we should see the light.
We see ourselves as helpless when we should call on God's might.

But, after all, we are only people and as such we fail many times.
That is why there are wars and stealing and all sorts of crimes.
Like Adam and Even as soon as God said to us don't.
The temptation to see why is too great. We should listen but we won't.

Until something happens to wake us from our state of mind
And we finally search for the Lord for total truth to find.
It seems we do everything the hard way here on Earth.
It starts from the very moment and day of our birth.
We are people!
God forgives us!

You know I have a problem that I work at everyday. It is easy to pass
judgment but when I do that I not only judge the one I am aiming at but also
myself. Before I tell you that I believe you are wrong, I must first look into
my own heart. What I find there makes me want to be more forgiving with
others.

Judge a Man by what you see in his Heart!

Do not judge a man by the color of his skin or way he worships God.
Do not think of him as sinful or dirty or even as if he was odd.
First, get to know him and find out what made him what he is today.

Do not be too quick to pass judgment upon the things you think you
heard him say.

Take some time to get to know him and try hard to understand.
Know him as someone who can be your friend and maybe one who
needs a helping hand.
Judge him by his ability to love and to accept the love of others.
Know that even if you have differences you are proclaimed by Christ to
be brothers.

Jesus said, "If any man asks anything of you, you are to freely give."
That includes the love you give as well as the ability to forgive.
So judge not your brother for as you do, you judge yourself as well.

If you are quick to proclaim their immortal death you may find
yourself in hell.
So love your neighbor as yourself and never, ever forget.
God sees what you accomplish and he will reward you as he sees fit.

The inevitable happens. Before long the very force which brings us together
drives crevices between us. Actually, the force that brings us together does
not do this. We do this. The Apostle Paul wrote that when we come
together, "each bring a prophecy." I truly think he meant point of view.
Since I am no better than you nor are you better then me, we each can learn
from our discussions if we can do so without judging. This seems to be a
problem with man since his very creation. Let us love one another.

Heartbreak

Would you like to know what tears at my heart and makes me want to
cry?

It is the fact that the one who died for us has been simply passed off
with a sigh.
He hung high on the cross to pay for our sins but we too often continue
to sin.
Each of us chooses to follow him in our own way claiming a prize to
win.

This should not surprise me for he said that this would come to pass.
Some speak in tongues, some go to Wednesday night meetings and
some simply go to mass.
We, each of us have chosen our path but somehow we too often forget.
The end of our journey is to take us each to Heaven with our Lord on
his thrown to sit.

He told us, "You think I came to bring peace, but I came to drive a
sword between you."
Little did we know the division would not simply be those who do not
believe in Jesus and those who truly do?
For the division that cuts through our religious world today is between
Gods very own.
We all believe in the same Jesus Christ but we place more emphasis on
what we condone.

We say, "You do not believe the way I do so you must be headed for
Hell."
We do not try to understand the things our brothers and sisters may
have to tell.
Is it any wonder that our Lords prophecy has come to pass as he told
it?
"There will be a great falling away from the truth," he said and he was
not kidding, not a little bit.

Why the falling away from the truth? Maybe it is because we have let
ourselves become divided one from the other.
We should not stress our differences so much as we should love one
another like Sister and Brother.

The Seed

Do you know what is funny about a seed? If you put it in the ground and it for any reason fails to draw nutrients from the soil, it dies. You say that is not funny? You are right. It is sad. Another seed is destroyed because it did not grow. There could be any number of reasons. Jesus said once, some of the seed was sewn upon the sand and it sprouted but when the drought came it quickly died. Some was sewn upon rock. It never had a chance. Biologically speaking it is possible that some was drowned by too much rain, causing it to rot.

Spiritually speaking, the word is planted upon each of our hearts. What we do with it is up to us. God gave us free will. Do you for one second think he didn't know what Adam and Eve would do as soon as he said don't? He knew they would exercise their free will and he knew there would be a price to pay but this leads for the better of us all. For centuries, now we have all been fighting that same battle. It is not a battle of nations, or a battle of groups, clicks, denominations of churches or any political battle.

It is a battle that each of us fights with himself. God knew this. Have you ever considered how the body's immune system becomes strong? It does so by working. We take antibiotics to help the immune system strengthen itself. What are antibiotics? They are weaker versions of the very germs or bacteria that cause flue, colds and other diseases.

I really believe God said, "let us make a test run for man and woman while they are still in the body. They will do exactly what I expected but only by learning from their great mistakes can they ever learn that free will and God's will are not a choice to make. Choose God of your own free will and you grow.

Now, let's get back to that seed. There it lies in the ground. It could live or die. It could reach for the warmth of the sun (God) or it could let itself be overcome with the fact that is buried and thereby simply become part of the fertilizer that will help other plants grow. If it reaches for the sun it will sprout through the ground and grow into a glorious plant.

Here is more food for thought. When it does sprout it will possibly be surrounded by any number of different plants. They live together in harmony. Each is growing and each reaching for the sun. Each creates oxygen for man to breath so they all share something else in common. They, each and every one have something to give.

Can we be like those plants? If we can, it will make our Lord so proud. He watches the ones who overcome the desires of the Earth and reaches for eternity. It is these ones that he was working for all the way back to the Garden of Eden.

God created us all. Male and female created he them. He meant for us all to give something to him. When we help a neighbor or even a stranger who is in distress we are doing so for God and he will praise us for it. After all, he is our Father.

Living for God is like chasing the sunset. You never quite make it. I have noticed that the sun sets too fast and before long there is another sunrise. God is like the Sun. His presence cultivates life. Not just life, but eternal life. I thank God for his presence and his love.

Chasing the Sunset

It is a long journey between birth and death
There are so many things that must happen between your first and last breath.

One thing I know about death and its sting
Is it not so much pain but a beautiful song to sing?

Sometimes it seems as if I am chasing the sunset.
I see it from far away but never up close and this is my regret.
My common sense tells that like life, when I touch the Sun
This will be symbolic that my earthly life is done.

So, though I chase the setting sun I am in no hurry.
My Lord walks with me while teaching me not to worry.
He touches my heart as the rays of the sun touch my skin.
He heals my soul of corruption and sin.

He loves me though I cannot figure out why.
But his love frees my soul as the Holy Spirit cleanses with a sigh.
He never lets me forget this love is forever.
He stands beside me through good times and bad and leaves me alone
never.

This is my faith and this is my song.
God teaches me each day what is right and what is wrong.
When I have learned all that he has to give
I will not need this life for in eternity will I live.

Someone asked me if I would rather live today when we do not respect our
elders, dress without modesty show not respect for the morals that we should
live by or in the past when we were perfect. We were respectful, didn't dare
dress immodestly and premarital sex was strictly forbidden. My answer is,
"I choose neither." I will live for the day when what we live will be honest
and from the heart because we will be in held in the arms of God.

Oh, for the Good Ole Days!

I have spent some time recollecting my memory of days gone by.
I have deliberated just what I see and why.

I must admit an awful lot of those memories are what I want to
remember.
Things like the glorious spring, the warm summers and Christmas in
December.

But if I am true to myself I must admit to this as I look back through
the years.
I was a child and wanted to do the things that would impress my piers.
I too often would compromise my character by the desire to be one of
them.
It is this desire which would many times stand between me and him.

You ask, "Who is HIM?" He is Jesus Christ, My Lord.
It was only when I got older that I picked up my spiritual sword
And struck down the very sin of my youth before it could grow.
Then I became more careful of the seeds that I sow.

It is now that I realize that the good ole days were not all as good as I
thought.
For I was still looking for something but did not always follow what I
was taught.
The good ole days were great in that I was young and full of life.
But they were also days that were truly full of strife.

It has been said, "In the good ole days, we respected our elders and
dressed with modesty."
In truth, we did to their face but would whine and curse them under
our breath,
Showing no hint of honesty.
A child does not understand the troubles that life can deal.
He does not realize the power of honesty to heal.

These things he learns as he grows older and wiser, day by day.
I have learned that the way of the Lord is the only true way.
Only when we receive him into our life and live it always
Can we truly say we will be with our Lord for the rest of our days.

Someone once said youth is wasted on the young and to that there is
some truth, indeed.
But like any young flower, we sprout from the seed.
We reach for our Lord like the flower reaches for the Sun.
Our blessing comes the day when we meet with God's Son.
It is sad that many people look for happiness but never find it. I wonder if
they did not find it because they were looking in all the wrong places. Lay
your burdens upon the Lord and true happiness will be yours.

Happiness!

I asked my Lord a question that had been heavy on my mind.
For though I searched all Earthly sources the answer I could not find.
How can I obtain happiness I asked him with all my heart?
This is the answer which My Heavenly Father did impart.

If you want to be truly happy that relieves the burdens of your mind
You must first search for the word and the happiness you will find.
"What means this?" I asked him for I did not know what he was telling me.
His answer was simple. "When you find it that is when you will see."

"How do I find the word?" I asked for I was now perplexed and confused.
"Search the scriptures and search your heart," he said. I asked for more but he refused.
So I went about this search but I knew not what I looked for.
Then I had a revelation which freed my mind and spirit.

The word was always with me though I could never hear it.
The word which I was looking for was not written, spoken or sung.
The word of God is Jesus Christ and as I said his name I noticed the bells had rung.
He is my first and last and all things in between.

He is the love of the father and of Heaven which is yet to be seen.
True happiness will not let disappointment dim its warm and brilliant glow.
For even in disappointment we learn and reach for our Lord and grow.
So put on your happy face, my friend and never dwell in sorrow.
For whatever you are dealing with today will build toward a better tomorrow.

Sadly, we all find ourselves too busy to really live. This is a problem that grows more and more every year. This is why we have so many health problems. This is why, even with modern medicine and all its wonders we too often do not lead happy lives. True happiness comes when we learn to enjoy the simplest pleasures. Watching those lazy clouds which flow gently overhead is a wonderful way to relax and thus lower your blood pressure and strengthen your heart to speak nothing of what it does for the spirit. Is it not a good thing to feel closer to God?

Things We Take for Granted

It is morning and sun rises in the east but that is nothing new.
The morning comes and soon its noon and on a good day the sky is blue.
Clouds will float peacefully across the sky but we often are to busy to see.
But when summer storms come upon us with thunder and lightning it awakens you and me.

The evening will bring the sunset in all its wondrous display of colors so bright.
The sad truth is that we too often are too busy to notice its beauty but only the dimming light.
Every day will come and go and what do we notice about it?
Only that we are growing older but not always wiser and thus we do not profit.

Tomorrow will bring another sunrise. Will we take the time to admire its glow?
Will we admire the clouds floating throughout the day and the sun as over the mountains it will go?
Will we thank the Lord for he has given us this life to live?
Will we see opportunities to share with others and in this way God's gift we will give?

Another day, another dollar... Sadly this has become our motto.
Have we considered that we are not thinking as we ought to?
Let us enjoy every sunrise and every sunset that God Gives.
And let us share his wonderful love with every single being that lives.

Have you noticed that I seem to write a lot of poems about autumn? I guess it is because autumn is a beautiful time of year. The next poem was inspired as I noticed that the days are shorter and the temperatures are falling in preparation of winter which will soon bring frost, snow and wind. I saw the leaves on the maple tree in front of our house shaking as if they were shivering in the cold. The real cold is yet to come but the leaves by then will be gone. Yet, even in this sight I cannot help but see Gods work

.

The Autumn Leaves Shiver

As I awoke this morning and looked out my window
I noticed it was not as light. Where did the summer go?
I saw the trees standing in the cool autumn air.
They were not standing still for their limbs shook everywhere.

I saw the leaves shivering in the cool breeze of autumn.
In the background I saw the darkened sky, a sight that was so
awesome.
For the sun had not yet cleared the mountains in the east.
The sky was gray a prisoner of the darkness, begging for release.

As the day grows on the gray stayed as if saying, "I have control for
now."
It is autumn and I know that winter will follow soon and as leaves
drop, the trees seem to bow.
For they will soon sleep throughout the cold winter months ahead.
It will seem at times as if they and the flowers have joined the dead.
What joy waits for us when spring comes to call them back to life
again.
A part of nature that reminds us of the resurrection and of Gods
forgiveness for sin.
So let us enjoy every season and every day of the year
For everyday that God gives us is a gift for us to hold dear.

I find the clouds intoxicating no matter what time of year. They seem
to move higher in the sky in autumn and then, just a quickly lower
themselves to create a ceiling above our heads. When you look from
one angle, you see white fluffy puffs of clouds that really do resemble
the breath of God. From another angle, especially as you find them
directly overhead they look like a gray ceiling hanging over you and
shutting out the sunshine. If you take the time to watch, this is a
beautiful pageant.

I See Clouds

I was driving home today and I watched the clouds which seemed to
move away.
But they were not moving away for I was driving under them on a cool
autumn day.
Yet it looked like they were running from me and my car.
It was as if they actually thought I could go where they are.

They were floating high in the heavens above
Protected by God and his almighty love.
Yet they seemed as if they thought they were being chased
As they floated above with a beauty too glorious to be erased.

I found myself calling to them to stay and paint the sky.
It was a beautiful picture resembling the breath of God given with a
sigh.
They mingled with each other and stood apart from the blue
stratosphere.
So fluffy and full like cotton candy but floating away as if in fear.

Eventually I drove under these beautiful pieces of God's creation.
The clouds grew darker and sky relented its color of blue as if in
agitation.
And as I drove on the sky was now gray for I had driven under the
clouds, then.
Autumn is like that. The weather changes so quickly and I watched the
work of the wind

It blew across the land and caressed the trees causing them to wave to
the sky.
The leaves were blowing from the trees, glancing across my windshield
as they flew by.
The day that started cloudy had become clear and bright
And then just as suddenly took on the essence of night.

Autumn is like that. It is a time of constant change of the atmosphere
It prepares the way for winter when we celebrate holidays with those
we hold dear.

Have you ever felt like God was far away and you try to bring him closer but
he seems to be avoiding contact? If so, have you ever thought that it may not
be God who is avoiding contact. It may be your own willful blindness. I
have! I know that whenever I feel that God has neglected me, I am wrong.
Those are the times when I have turned from him. I will feel the loneliness
until I turn back to my Savior.

Seeing Through Earthly Eyes

Where are you Lord, for I cannot see?
But I hear your words... you speak to me.
If I cast my eyes in your direction
They are immediately blinded by your brilliant reflection.

How can I see you if I am blinded by your light?
This could, indeed be my greatest plight.
These were questions that I once asked of you.
Until one day I found the answer true.

I watched the waves of the ocean break.
I saw the first morning light as the world did awake.
I saw you in the leaves hanging on the trees
And I felt you in the early morning breeze.

You are the clouds and the sky of blue.
You are the colors of autumn when the summer is through.
You are in every snowflake which floats from the sky.
These are all things to behold with human eye.

You are here and there and everywhere.
I see you in mountain lake or the desert dry and bare.
You show yourself in so many ways.
Each part of nature proclaims your power throughout my days.

Where are you Lord, for I cannot see?
This is a question lame and it reflects on me.
For if I cannot see you it is my own blindness which punishes my spirit.
If I can look I can see and if I listen for your voice I will hear it.

Life has thrown some horrible curves my way but God has given me strength to overcome them and keep my faith. Part of that strength is found in the love of my wife whose love is an extension of God's caring and preparing. Praise God for all good things.

An Angel Sent from God

When she smiles my face immediately lights.
She gives me encouragement to overcome any plight.
Her voice is soft and sweet and kind.
She is the most loving, gentle and understanding wife a man could find.

No, she does not have wings and she cannot fly
But when I am with her the one taking wings am I.
God knew what I needed even before I understood.
He sent me this Angel to stand beside me through bad times as well as
good.

How can I ever repay her wonderful love?
How can I ever repay this wonderful God up above?
The answer is so simple that I have stopped asking how.
The answer is I can't. So, when at night I bow
Before my God and my Savior I thank him for his love.
Part of which is this angel whose love came from above.

It is sad but when we get behind the wheel of our car we tend to become
competitive. You hear about road rage. This happens when a driver
becomes so incensed by what he considers to be the heartless act of another
that he does something foolish. This sometimes ends up with two wrecked
cars and possibly someone injured or dead. I have become aware of the fact
that we do not always have traffic lights at every intersection or every
shopping mall. People can become so impatient that they try something
foolish. I would rather motion them into the lane in front of me rather than
have a catastrophe.
That is why I wrote the next poem.

Driving for Christ

If we truly love our Lord and Savior we show it in all we say and do.
That includes how we love our family with a love that's pure and true.
It causes us to expand our family to friends and neighbors and even
strangers.
We protect these people as much as possible from all of life's horrid
dangers.

Have you ever thought that it also affects the way we drive our car
each day?
If we compete with others for the better lane of traffic are we living our
lives Gods way?
A smile on your face and a tap on your horn will let the other drivers
know.
That you are willing to help them out and you will wait for them to go.
One good deed inspires another and if you can start with that one good
deed
Maybe it will touch someone's heart and soul and he will help others in
need.

The love of God is shown in everything we say and do.
So you see, this is a good way to forward the love to another as a gift
freely given from you.
Slow down and live. Give the right-a-way make God's love part of
your style.
You will live a better life on Earth and you will see Heaven with a
smile.

When I awoke this morning I saw the beginning of a gray and rainy day.
The day has not brightened much at this point and it looks like rain is in the
forecast. This does not bother me for into every life a little rain must fall.
Jesus said, "The rain falls on the just and the unjust. This was more like a
reminder to me that God works in silence and unseen by human eyes but if
your spirit is tuned in you will feel his presence.

When I awoke

When I awoke this morning the sky was dark and gray.
I saw no rising sun to brighten up my day.
However, though I could only see its light as if through dense and dark clouds.
I still welcomed the rising sun and praised God with a voice so loud.

The Sun may not be shining with its entire brilliant glow
But it is still rising, shining on the clouds, of this I truly know.
Yes, my friend there will be cloudy days of only semi-light.
However, though the Sun is not visible it still interrupts the night.

God is like that, you know. We do not see him though he is always there.
We have no idea what he may look like but we know he will always care.
So when you have those days when the skies are dark and gray
Remember that God's almighty love goes with you every day.

Believe in him and live your life as if you truly know
That God is with you all the time and everywhere you go.

When I was growing up, we were told there was a Communist behind every bush. We were taught the duck and cover method thing in school. In case of an ever impending atomic attack get under your desk and cover your eyes. The attack never came and the Communists are no more. This generation is watching for terrorists. This is good. We need to watch for them. But, what if you're looking in all the wrong places and overlooking those who terrorize our youth?

Do You Fear Them?

There are those who would have us fear terrorists
But I ask you to consider this.
A terrorist can be anybody for they walk within our mists.
The guy who speeds past you going way over the speed limit
He is a terrorist, too.

The person who loses his temper and strikes his wife
He is a terrorist, too.

The man or woman who cares not that there are children at play as
they drive, endangering their life
They are terrorists, too.

A terrorist does not necessarily use bombs, guns or fly planes into
buildings that are tall.
They can be more subtle and simply live heartless lives, following no
conscience at all.
They care not for anyone but themselves, their own desires to appease.
If they cause danger to another, they have become one of these.

A terrorist can be your next door neighbor, you see.
They could even be you or me.
Let us live our lives knowing the love of Jesus Christ, our Lord.
Then the true terrorist of them all will be defeated, his hatred cut with
God's holy sword.

Satan has no power over us that we do not give him of our own free
will.
Are you relinquishing that power to him? Does he control you life
still?
I pray you are drawing from the power of a wonderful God who loves
us every one.

A love that is reflected through Jesus who hung on that cross till our
battle was won.
He won it for you and me. He paid the price for our many sins.
He who accepts the gift is the person who finally wins.
Heaven is waiting. Are you ready to see it?

Do you know what the sadist thing about man is? We have a tendency to
turn to God only in the middle of a catastrophe. We do not follow him as
closely when life is going well. We tend to thank ourselves for our successes.
Only when we find ourselves feeling alone do we turn to the Lord for

comfort. Isn't it such a waste? We should thank God for every breath, every, heartbeat and yes for everything we accomplish in this life. It would all be so meaningless without him.

Deep Feeling

I sometimes have this feeling dwelling deep down inside.
I feel like I want to run; I feel like I want to hide.
I ask myself the question, "What am I hiding from?"
Fear beats through my soul like the sound of a beating drum.

When I ask myself if there is a reason
I find none, for it comes in any season.
The fear is something I feel when I stray from God's path.
I think the fear is that I will one day know his wrath.

But why did I stray from his beautiful way?
Why is it that I am tempted to stray?
For the pathway he sent me on leads to eternal glory.
Knowing that tomorrow, today will simply be history.

He guides me when I follow his lead.
Yet, there are times when I feel that to follow I do not need
I do not require his lead and guidance to see me through.
His love and compassion sometimes is simply not appreciated
And our souls at these times are truly depreciated.
God's wrath comes slow and love endures.
He saves my soul and he will save yours.

Have you ever noticed that we all tend to have self pity parties? We do. I do and I am sure I am not alone. When we find ourselves saying, "Oh woe is me," we doubt the love of our creator. He knows when life seems hard. He shares the hardship. He can deliver us from our own worst enemy. That is very often our self. So let us not dwell in pity but praise God for every breath for it is a gift from him.

Why Are You Sad?

Why are you sad, my little one?
Why are there tears in your eyes?
Why does your heart carry such a horrible burden?

Your sadness is wasted, but true love is wise.
Love me as your savior and your neighbor as your brother.
Know my love binds you together, a love like no other.

Why do you insist on bringing heartbreak into your life?
What is accomplished by living your life in spiritual strife?

I can relieve the sadness and replace it with a greater love.
I can give comfort to you which is my gift from above.
Jesus hung on that cross for each one who turned to him.
He paid a price for your sins and brought brightness that will never
dim.
Do not shield your eyes from it but bask in its luster.
Praise the Lord thy God with all the spiritual energy you can muster.

Gods love is forever so why do you not hold fast?
When your earthly life is over, eternity will still last.

Turn to Jesus Christ and you will know God!

As I look back on my life, mixed in with wonderful memories like the
day I met my wife and the birth of each of my children and grandchildren
there are some memories that are not as happy. Some of them were
heartbreaking things that happened to me personally but a lot of them are
things I wish I had or had not done or said. I think we all are aware of these.
Have you ever wondered if things would have been better if you could change
certain things? We probably all have. Well, the truth is we cannot relive the
past but we still have a future. Let us make God a part of it.

Missed Opportunities

The years have truly taken their toll
And they came and they went by as if on a roll.
Now I see the reflection in the mirror of man grown old.
I am no longer the young scamp who always felt self-assured and bold.
Now as I look back I have wonderful memories.
Amidst them, I must admit there are some sad stories.
Times when I could have made a powerful change the life of another.
But, alas I was too wrapped up in myself to care enough for my
brother.
Now, I look back and wish I could live it all again
That way, I could fine tune my life and see things done as they should
have been.
My Lord and master will not allow me to live this life anew.
But his forgiveness washes away those sins and failures and he can do
the same for you.
He does ask of us one thing, though. He asks us to honestly admit our
past and present sin.
Once we do this, he will be forgiving and honorable and allowed us to
start again.
Learn from the mistakes you make each day and we all will surely do
so.
Then lay those problems on God's shoulders as through each day we
go.
Christians are not perfect. Christians are forgiven!

The story is true and I am now watching through my windows as our
Dogwood bush puts on a beautiful show. There are no blossoms for it is fall.
But in the fall the tree's leaves are every bit as beautiful. Life is renewable.
Believe and you can be a part.

We Mourn No More

We were young and love and preparing to marry.
We searched for a house in which to make merry.
We found a modest home in a nice neighborhood.
It was not huge but we knew it would serve us good
In the front yard there stood a pink dogwood tree.
Its blossoms were full and standing proudly for all to see.
In the fall we found another pleasant surprise.
The blossoms had fallen of but something else caught our eyes.
The leaves turned a color of the most beautiful ruby red.
Two years ago, our beloved Dogwood was dead.
Many said it was a blight that caused it to wilt and die.
So, I cut down the tree with a sad and lonely sigh.
We cut the limbs off but we kept the stump standing a foot high.
My wife put a flower pot on top of the stump as a beautiful ornament.
Last spring we saw sprouts coming from around the stump and we
knew what that meant.
The dogwood tree would live once more to ordain our lawn.
What a wonderful joy to know that it was not gone.
Some say the dogwood is symbolic of Jesus hanging on the cross.
If he had not done so, this would have truly been our loss.
Just as he died and was raised from the dead
This is exactly what our pink dogwood tree did.
It is truly a symbol of the life recreated anew.
Though it was dead the Dogwood now stands proud and true.
Just as our lord, it shows that death has no hold on you or on me.
God has created life where death used to be.

This is not something that I simply thought would be beautiful to write. It is
about three plants in our front yard. Death became life and life begets life.
It seems our Dogwood is truly a symbol of our Lord and Savior Jesus Christ.
God in all his wisdom shows himself in so many ways that it is a shame that
any man could fail to see him and his love.

About That Dogwood

Something I had not noticed until today.
I told about the Dogwood tree, which we thought had gone away.
It came back and sprouted with beauty, luster and elegance.
Today I noticed something more, this story to enhance.
In the corner of our yard now grows another Dogwood tree.
In the opposite corner of the yard grows another that I see.
Where we once had one Dogwood, now it seems that we have three.
I mentioned the Dogwood was symbolic of Jesus hanging on the cross.
He came to save you and me and all those who were lost.
If the Dogwood was symbolic before today it is even more so now.
It shows us that the resurrection of our savior is imparted to us
somehow.
The Dogwood died and rose up from the dead again.
Now it has a church of followers who will stand with it till the end.
However the end is not really the end for it is the new beginning for all.
I see Jesus coming through the clouds with the trumpets mighty call.
Our little church of Dogwoods is steadily growing every day.
I pray that it will keep growing in every possible way.
I also pray that we have become followers of our Lord.
He is the one who freely died for us, the one who deserves to be adored.

I think it is so wonderful to hear a child pray. But it is even greater to watch them grow into adulthood and realize that the things they prayed for as children were only a part of learning to know the Master better. That is why I wrote the next poem. I truly hope you enjoy it. I think back about the prayers I prayed as a child. My life revolved around my mother and father, sister and brothers. It revolved around playing games and having a weekly allowance. It was based on simple things. I had no idea of just how complicated life could be. Now I am a father of three and a grandfather of five. I see life through their eyes with also from a different perspective.

Prayer Evolves

When we were young we were taught to say our daily prayers.
They were more like a letter to Santa than about our worries or cares.
Dear God, protect Mommy and Daddy and my Dog named Rover.
We would find ourselves praying for the same things over and over and over.
As we grow older, we hopefully learn to fine tune our devotions.
We praise to the Lord and thank the Lord and share with him our emotions.
Our prayers are not repeatedly pleading for this or for that or whatever.
Our prayers become more a "Thank you Lord," for I know you leave my side never.
As we grow in the Lord we realize that if we need it, he already knows.
We begin to understand we need not ask for anything and that's when our faith grows.
Now our prayers are conversations with our greatest and dearest friend.
He will always be there with us and give us strength all the way to the end.
When that end comes to pass, we will learn something more to add to our faith, indeed.
If ever we have asked for anything and he did not provide, it was something we did not need.
So remember when you pray to God, pray like Jesus taught and do not plead.
Our Father who art in Heaven, how holy is your name.
Thy kingdom come, thy will be done in Heaven and on Earth the same.
Remember when you ask of God, he already knows of what it is you ask.
The greatest gift he gives to us is faith to finish any task.

Have you ever considered how we can trap ourselves in the past? We probably all do it. Something about the past drives us to dwell on it and we never seem able to pull ourselves away from this. It could be a scar left from an unhappy event or it may be that there are wonderful memories that we don't want to let go of. I think it is wonderful to have those memories as long as we realize they are memories. Today has the potential of creating more memories but we need to keep ourselves focused on living today. Yesterday, be it a happy one or a heartbreaking one is over and those memories are all that is left. Today is where we are and tomorrow is yet to be lived. Trust in God and dare to dream. Today can be the beginning of a better tomorrow.
Put it where it belongs!

The past holds some unhappiness and this is like a heavy weight.
We must unload the burden which it imposes before it is too late.
We must accept the things that already are and start our life today.
We need to lay the burden of broken dreams on God and ask him to show the way.

The way he will show us is built on now and this leads us to our future.
If we trust in God everything about our days are a constant sequence of adventure.
Yesterday is gone and there is no way to go back and change it.
Today is here and is a first step to a future with God, Jesus and the Holy Spirit.
So put you're past aside and keep only what you have learned.
If there is sadness, like an end of a love affair that has left you feeling spurned
These can all be lifted from your shoulders to the stronger shoulders of God above.
He can carry these burdens for you with his never ending love.
The past has no place in the present unless we have learned something from it.
But if we refuse to leave it behind we have dug an eternal pit.
In that pit we are prisoners, the escape from which we have no hope at all.
Until the day we declare, I free myself by answering my Masters call.

When I was a child I spoke like a child. I reasoned like a child and I even prayed as a child. But when I grew older I put away my childish things and started to broaden my mind. Don't get me wrong. I am certainly no Saint. I make mistakes, even today. As I look back to my childhood I remember singing praises to Jesus because of what he could give me. The whole worship service revolved around me. I now know that I am not the center of the universe. If I do well for others it is not me working but God working through me. I will give him the praise.

Don't Be an Impersonator!

Are you a true follower of Christ, if so how does it show?
Even more important to you my friend is do you honestly within your
own heart know?
Here is a question that I ask myself over and over again.
If I follow the Ten Commandments is that a complete lack of sin?

If I give all what I have to the poor, that in itself earns me no place in
Heaven
Unless I give it because of a true love of God, Jesus and of my brethren.
What I am trying to convey to you is motive means more than the deed.

If we follow our Lord, do well to others and feed and house those who
are in need
This is a good thing and it is our Fathers wish that we would serve him
thus.
But he wants to look within our hearts and he asks, "What is it that
you lust?"
To make my point a bit clearer it was written in the word that works
alone was useless
Unless it is motivated by a true love for God and others and not simply
so we are blessed.
Give to the poor but remember that God has given us what we have to
give.

So when we give we are only passing on his gift to us. For this we
should strive to live.
So, my friend, do not impersonate a Christian. Be what you can be.
Until the day Jesus comes through the clouds taking the hands of you
and me.

Do you know what is funny about knowing Jesus Christ and through him knowing God, the Father? Everything you do becomes spiritual. Such peace and joy from anything and everything is a wonderful gift. This next poem started out to be an exclamation of a beautiful Saturday. As I wrote I felt compelled to thank the one who made it so. The next thing I knew I was praising God again. This is not a problem. This is a blessing. Whenever you look at the sky, with or without clouds, every time you admire the stars at night or take in the beauty of a full moon keep this in mind. God put them all there. He put us all here. He is here with us, over us, within us and loving us. Isn't that wonderful?

Crisp Saturday Joy

I awoke this morning feeling rested and full of joy.
I know this will be a Saturday to enjoy.
The air is crisp and the sky is a beautiful pale blue.
There is not a cloud in the sky, not even a few.

I know they will come back but today I simply admire the day.
I watch as the soft cool breeze causes the trees to sway
This way and that way as they keep up with the wind
They are shedding their leaves which drop and flow wherever the
breeze may send.

I see my Masters work everywhere I look and I thank God for his love
for my faith cannot be shook.
I will praise him and serve him as best I can serve.
I will swim in the pool of his love, a love I do not deserve.
But who am I to walk away from what he offers to me.

If he did not want me to have it I would surely never see
The wonder of all that he has created to be admired by us all
And the joy he gives and all blessings both large and small
I will admire the blue sky and feel the cool breeze as it caresses my
cheek

I will thank him for without his love I know I am very weak.
I will enjoy the sun while it shines and relish in the cool autumn air.
And know that God's love will overcome my each and every care.
Praise God who sends us the wind and also sends the rain.
Who knows all our troubles and feels our every pain.
Let God be our total source of strength.

When I wrote the 2004 upcoming elections were on everybody's mind as. We watched the news and we heard the statistics. This candidate is leading by four points or the presidents' approval is at an all time low. I won't get into politics for each man has a right to make up his own mind who he will vote for. What I will say is this. How do we know that any of them will keep their promises for a better tomorrow? The answer is, "We don't." So I will vote for the candidate of my choice but my future is in greater hands. My true vote is for Jesus Christ and the Father of us all. To our Dear old Uncle Sam, we are just a number. That's sad. God looks beyond that. He looks deep into our soul. Do you love him?

Statistics!

Are we just a one in a number of millions on the Earth?

Are we nothing more than math from the day of our birth?
Can our lives be subtracted as quickly as it was created?
Possibly, it is more than number related.

Perhaps, it means more than statistics and government polls.
Let us look at our lives as a gift from the creator.
Is our existence a number that is here today but will be gone later?
If all we represent is a number we are nothing more than math.

This means we are incapable of feeling Gods love or recognizing his
wrath.
Let the government play with their numbers if to do so they feel they
must.
Let us look above toward the one true God whom we know that we can
trust.
We can trust him to know our heartbreaks and we know he will feel
our pain.

Even during the sad times we know his love will still remain.
He sees us as his own and he wants our soul to be saved.
He even wants to forgive us when we have misbehaved.
So, my friend I share this wonderful and powerful thought with you.

God is with you wherever you go and with you whatever you do.
When you do well, it is because you have been wise to follow his lead.
When you fall, he will help you stand up again, straight and proud
indeed.

For his love for you is a never ending love.
One day we will all be with him in his kingdom, Heaven above.

Put not your faith in principalities but in the hands of the Lord.

My mind likes to travel now and then to yesteryear! I remember something
about my childhood that my kids would never believe. Grocery stores,
department stores and even restaurants were closed on the Sabbath. I guess
that is what made the Sunday dinner which we ate at noon so important to
us. The difference is you didn't call it lunch on Sunday. Today, everything
keeps going. No day of rest for the weary. Sunday is simply another day.
It's kind of sad. That is what prompted me to write the next poem.

Never on Sunday

In six days the Lord created the heavens and the Earth.
He double checked them and ascertained their worth.
On the seventh day he took some time to rest.
On this day he knew now that he had done his best.

Jesus admonished us to remember the Sabbath day and keep it holy in
Gods name.
He wanted us to take a day of rest, ourselves praising God in holy
refrain.
We have become more materialistic in this day and age.
I have often wondered, "Does this not cause God to shout with holy
rage?"

He asked that we keep the Sabbath and use it for rest and worship.
But, I guess our worship includes Wal-Mart and extended days of
salesmanship.
I wonder what our Master will say when we see him face to face.
Will he say we have profaned a Holy day and thereby laid it to waste?

The answers are not always clear for us to understand.
We live in the twenty-first century far from the Holy land.
Things change as the years go by and so does our worship service.
All the same, sometimes it all worries me and makes this old man
nervous.

Let us all dig within our hearts and pray for his insight.
Our days are numbered and our eyes will soon forced to see the night
When Jesus comes in the clouds as the Angels sing their sweet song.
Let us pray he finds we have not all gone completely wrong.

I spend a lot of time enjoying my grandchildren these days. I love my kids
but their lives are their own now so I just support them in whatever way I
can and pray for them constantly. I watch my wife as she feeds the
grandchildren much in the same way she fed our kids. This is what
prompted me to write the following poem. I am moved by the fact that I
sometimes wonder how the years have fled so quickly leaving only memories.

Fly, Fly Away

Birds fly high in the sky.
Each day of life takes flight as it skips by.
Then weeks take flight and are soon part of my past.
Then come the months winging past way too fast.

Finally as I look back I realize that years have gone for they could not last.
Now I find myself looking back on a life which I hope I lived well.
I have many memories and this means lots of stories to tell.
Once I was a child at play yearning to become grown-up and on my own.

Then I graduated high school and my life entered a new zone.
I should have been happy but somehow I felt all alone
Until the day I met her, and she became my source of joy.
Two years later we had a healthy baby boy.

Two girls followed and before I knew it I was a grandpa.
To say the least, my life has not been dull.
My life has been like that of a bird in flight.
I have gained much over the years including better insight.

Now as I live my days, months and years.
I look back at the times of joy and the periods of tears.
I also treasure each day ahead for I know.
Those days will come and how quickly they will go.

Live every day as a day unto the Lord, thy God above
And forget not the wonderful treasure that is founded in his great love.

In my home town there is a creek that runs around this small community
and on downstream where there are periods of calm water, seemingly not
moving and other places on further downstream where it is running fast and
furious. It empties into a river which is much the same as the creek but
wider and at places even more furious. The river, like the creek has places
where the water is calm and peaceful. My Dad used to take us fishing in
these still waters. That is what inspired the next write.

The River of Life

I stand on the bank of the river looking into the water, seemingly moving slow if at all.
I turn and look upstream where the water runs with fury over a rock break creating a falls.
I find myself drawn back to the tranquility of the water where I stand.
I see the bottom of the river, the water magnifying the fish that swim close to the banks where begins the land.

Then I turn and look downstream where the water is once more running.
The rippling falls and the white foam it creates is a view which is quite stunning.
Life is like that river, you know. Life sometimes runs furious and fast.
And other times it is quiet and complacent but these times do not last.

Tomorrow is another day and it may be quite a race.
It may take all of ones energy to try to keep the pace.
The quiet water in front of me represents today, the here and now.
Those falls upstream represent yesterday but it came to an end somehow.

Downstream is tomorrow but I will let it come as it may.
For right now, I have the present so I will live for today.
Whatever tomorrow brings my way, be it calm or fast moving currents running swiftly on.
I will trust in God for what the future holds and live today before it is gone.

The river moves sometimes at breakneck speed and sometimes seems not to move at all.
I hear it ripple as it moves downstream and I can hear the rivers call.
I also hear my master calling for me to come home to him.
The rippling waters suddenly sound sweet like a beautiful and holy hymn.

Praise god for the river and praise him for the sky and praise him for the sea.
Praise him for Jesus Christ who died on the cross for you and me.

I have found a cure for depression. Jesus Christ! He is my tie with God. Here is someone who I can take my problems to. As I talk with him those problems become less heartbreaking and I find myself praising him for life. Prayer is a communication with our Lord and savior. No limits on monthly minutes. No charge for long distance and it is a long way to Heaven. Oh... and one more thing. There are no dropped calls.

Oh Whoa Is Me!

If I be without the grace of Jesus Christ our Lord
Oh, whoa is me!

If I put my faith in principalities of the world
Oh, whoa is me!

If I hear the word of God but do not live it with all my might
And have not my light trimmed with his flame to help me through the
night
Oh whoa is me!

If I find I have no forgiveness for others if they have done me wrong.
If I cannot lay my hurt upon the shoulders of my God to him I do not
belong.
Oh whoa is me!

If his love has changed my life causing me to love my sisters and my
brothers.
If his love reflects within my life and thereby glows to others
I am thereby freed from sin and doubt and made ready for his
forgiveness.
I thereby am a disciple of his and will be lead by his loving goodness.

If I have learned to serve my Lord and follow his commandments as I
have learned them.
I thereby learn to know him better and will move ever closer to him.
If I have learned these things and keep them in my heart
Oh, whoa is me is not my lament for I now have a new start.

This morning I went to the grocery store. There was a lady driving one of
those power carts for she obviously could not walk but she drove in the
middle of isle so I could not squeeze by. I found myself feeling a little put
out. Then she noticed me there and excused herself and moved the cart to
the side. As I passed I said thank-you and she smiled. As I thought about
this I began to dwell on the fact that we are all in too great a hurry. We feel
we have no time to show courtesy. This is why I wrote this poem.
What Ever Happened

What ever happened to courtesy?
Have we all grown much to busy?
Does it take something away from our self esteem?
If we say please and thank you, does it make us seem
As if we are weak and timid if we take the time to say
Things like please, thank-you or give someone a smile each day?

We drive like the other drivers have no heart
In a rat race in which we, ourselves are a part.
Do we think of our neighbor is the guy who lives next door?
But he is someone we would rather ignore?

Why do we feel the need to cut ourselves off from others?
These people are all our sisters and brothers.
If we believe in Christ do we not believe his words?
Do we read the good book but soon forget it afterwards?

If you have found yourself saying yes to what is written above.
You should pray to God to help you cultivate agape love.
Then when you learn to love in his name
You will find the love you receive back is the same.

It is the same love that led Jesus to the cross.
To not live for him would be our greatest loss.
Love ye one another.

This is an experiment. What I did was set down with a pencil. Imagine that, a pencil and not my computer. I wrote down names and words that rhymed and then tried to make them into a poem. Mind you, the poem had no place to go unless I could fit the names and words into it. Then I started building around them.

Mary and Sherry
There were two ladies by the name of Mary and Sherry
Sherry had too many burdens to carry.
Sherry was depressed so Mary worked hard trying to make Sherry merry.
She told of a fellow named Stew.

Who found himself feeling quite blue.
No matter how he tried to pull himself up he didn't know what to do.
Sherry explained to Mary that she could be like the wind.
It blows whenever it wants and never comes to an end.

Her advice to Mary was to reflect on things like a star filled night in June.
"Look around you my Dear sweet Sherry" said Mary "and take time to admire the moon".
Do not be like Frank for his greatest joy is pulling a nasty prank
And be not like Jane for she suffers with pain what she sees around her with great distain.

Be ye not afraid to let joy cause your spirit to have great fun
Dwell on happiness, peace of mind and great joy can be won.
Do not spend your whole life in worry
But work for the good of God, be busy and scurry.

Take your time and build on your life, there is no hurry.
Only then will you will have then gained peace of mind.
You can reach out to friends for they are the tides that bind.
Dwell not on you troubles but look to help others and be sensitive and always kind.

Said Sherry I will try this for it sounds like love.
I will embrace this love and place it high above
Everything else that I do and I will start with you.

Jesus is quoted in the gospels as saying, "You think I have come to bring peace but I have come to drive a sword between brothers." I truly believe he said this because he knew us so well. We have spent all of history fighting amongst ourselves. We have fought wars causing many innocent lives to be destroyed. Do you truly believe God did not know of our need for power, money and easy living? Do you honestly believe that he thought our desire for unity with him would not be costly to us in this world? I think he knew. He knows what we live with and he also knows what our reward is. Let us be one with God and that means let us be one with one another.
Put away Thy Sword

"Why do you fight amongst yourselves?" Our Savior quietly asks.
"Can you not make your love for me and for one another greatest among life's tasks?"
He also asks us to search our hearts and bring ourselves to accept his love.
For if we truly accept his love we will surely be lifted above.

We will be lifted above hatred, bigotry, self-righteousness and sin.
For his love is our only salvation to make us one with him again.
What keeps the Christian faith from growing in this sinful world today?
The answer is the lack of unity. Division causes us all to stray.

How is it that those who do not believe can demoralize us this way?
The answer is that we have allowed it because together we do not stay.
If we believe in Jesus Christ we may have different understanding.
He will forgive us when we make wrong decisions for his love is not demanding.

So let us not separate ourselves or alienate ourselves from him or one another.
Let us love each other and join together treating others like sister in brother.
For in the eyes of Christ, he who forgives will also be forgiven.
That forgiveness is a one way ticket to a place that we call Heaven.

Jesus summed up the Ten Commandments into two. He came to simplify and he did. "Love the Lord thy God with all thy heart and all thy soul and thy entire mind and love thy neighbor as thyself." I don't believe he meant do this and you have salvation. I think he meant if you have salvation, you will do this. So the Ten Commandments or the short version spoken of above mean, if I find myself not doing this, I need to pray to God for I do not yet know him as I should.

Today

Today, you know was yesterday's tomorrow!
It is tomorrow's yesterday carrying memories of happiness as well as sorrow.
As tomorrow becomes today it creates a new tomorrow.
Our time on Earth must be more than something we simply borrow.

So what of this thing called passage of time?
Is it simply a slow voyage with not one reason or rhyme?
What of this life we live through all our today's"?
Why is it that our yesterday never stays?

What do we look for in our tomorrow or all the days that come?
Are they simply a constant beat of a distant drum?
Do we make the most of each day we live?
Do we find the time to care and to give?

To those who are needy and poor and deceased?
When our today is yesterday can we feel that we have eased?
Their pain and given them hope?
Have we simply lived selfishly for ourselves as we blindly grope.

Do we search for anything to foster our own sense of comfort?
Is it possible we just do want to make an effort?
Or can we possibly change someone's tomorrow?
Bring happiness into their lives and cast out their sorrow.

This would also make a glorious change for all our todays.
Today becomes tomorrow morning and sees the first of the suns rays.
A brighter today made by something you did yesterday.
This, my friend is God's Holy way!

How many of us can honestly say we have never felt as if we had lost ourselves? I would guess that if any of us are honest we would have to say there were times. We, after all are only human. We are prone to make mistakes and we are apt to do and say things that we know we should not do or say. That is why God's wonderful forgiveness is such a glorious gift. Keep in mind, though that we need to realize how badly we need that forgiveness. He will not thrust it upon us. He will ask until we admit our need for it. That is called confession.

How Did I Get Here?

I once thought I had my life in total control.
I had my plans ready and I thought I was on a roll.
The strangest thing about the way that I see things now
Is that I lost track of where I was heading somehow.

Oh how grateful I am to my Master
Without his wonderful love my life could have become a major
disaster.
I took some wrong turns and found that I had lost the way.
Tired and alone, I walked through the darkness of that day.

God turned on a light leading me out of the blackness.
His strong arms reached for me to overcome my weakness.
"Are you ready now to follow my guide," he asked quietly.
I nodded and humbly bowed my head silently.

How did I ever lose my way? I wondered in confusion.
God answered, "The control of your life was nothing more than an
allusion.
For life takes many twists and numerous turns.
As one lives in humility then that same person learns

That the Master of your fate is the one by which you were created.
This is the truth and it should not be debated.
So give the control of your life over to me.
If you will follow, I will lead you across the widest sea.

To the home that will never allow you to be lost and depressed.
For in my kingdom, love, light and joy means you'll never be
depressed.
Follow my Son and he will lead you home beyond the clouds.
Where the music you hear will be praises sung loud.

Love is kind and gentle. Love is forgiving. Love does not hold grudges.
Love endures all things. Love overcomes all things and most of all love gives
us the ability to care for one another just as our Heavenly Father loves each
of us. Will you accept his love?

Love

Love is a wonderful source of happiness and joy.
Love can also be painful and be a cause to annoy
The person who loves if that love is not returned in kind.
Love is something that grows in the heart and then to the mind.

There are those who avoid this thing called love for it can cause pain.
It can create heartache and with each beat of the heart those feelings
refrain.
If I never loved I may avoid the hurt and the trauma.
It may save me from living through the horrible drama.

I may spare myself the anxiety of wondering if my love is returned.
I never will worry if I will find that I have burned.
On the other hand if I hide from the dangers of caring
And never allow myself to feel carefree and daring.

If I do not allow myself to make myself vulnerable
I will find that I have not found my intentions to be honorable.
What if Jesus had not loved us with such love that he did?
What if he had come to simply condemn us instead?

If you have never loved your life will be empty and without grace.
You will never know the joy of sharing whatever life gives you to face.
So be brave, my friend and love with all your heart.
Learn to know God and his kingdom so that you may be a part.

"For God so loved the world that he gave his only begotten son that who so
ever believeth in him should not perish for have everlasting life."
I wrote the following poem because I am a grandfather. I have wondered
how the CEO's of the giant oil companies and any others that pollute our
Earth can live with the knowledge that their children and grandchildren are
going to pay the price for their great success. The question is, 'if it is
destroying our Earth, can they really call it a success?'

When a Baby Smiles

When he smiles I can see teeth that are brand new.
I see the sparkle in his eyes come shining through.
That sparkle no doubt is reflected in my own eyes, I'm sure.
He reaches for me and I cuddle him close to reassure.

I am not sure what his future will bring.
I know not whether as he grows older he will see the spring.
At least, I am not sure he will see it like I have as a child.
It was a wondrous time when the breezes were soft and mild.

The air seemed clearer and the sky was bluer to me.
Possibly that, though is just because these old eyes do not see.
My grandchildren will live in a time when global warming is news.
The price they will pay because our generation will abuse.

And these, along with generations before have been changing the
Earth.
Stripping it of its natural resources and dimensioning its worth.
We need to think of our children and their grandchildren and then
theirs.
We need to work for a better, cleaner Earth before a destructive wind
stirs

It will give our descendents a world full of pollution.
Then one day there will be no hint of a solution
Things will become more lethal with toxic fumes so impure.
Our children and their grandchildren will be unable to endure.

Tell the people in power that this is important not only to us but to
those who come after.
Let's work together so that our children will find comfort and
laughter.
God put man in charge of taking care of Earth.
Let us stand up and declare with all that we are worth

That now is the time to clean up the air,
The water and soil. Let us show that we care.
If we do not our decedents will pay for our sins.
Let us all work till a new Earth begins.

I have not been to the ocean for quite a while but something caused me to dwell on happy days when a day at the ocean was my greatest joy. I have seen many changes taking place in my lifetime. Now there are violent storms. The Earth has grown warmer due to the greenhouse affect. There are many people who argue whether man had anything to do with it or if it was just a part of the Earths constant changing. Either way, we need to be careful how we treat the planet for we know not how long God intends for us to stay here.

The Oceans Tides

I have wonderful memories that go back to childhood days.
They once were vivid but are now they are seen as in a haze.
The ocean tide comes washing ashore.
It washes upon the sand and followed by one more.

The tide seems to wash away the sand
But somehow the next wave comes to land
It replaces the sand that was moved off shore.
As I watched over the white crest of each wave I could see more.

They never stop their constant movement and their energy never dies.
If I look far enough over the wave I see the skies.
The clouds just above the water are misty and gray.
It seems as if by the water they are content to stay.

Higher up in the sky the color is blue and the sun shines bright.
Soon comes the sunset followed by the night.
Then goes on the constant singing of the oceans cry
It's a relaxing chant to my ears as I study the stars in the sky.

The waves come and go but they are followed by more.
They wash in and rush out but others are in store.
We need to protect this for it is one of Gods greatest creations.
The waves come and go to all of Earths nations.
Don't pollute!

I know something that comforts me more than I can say. God is more than a person, an entity, he is a power. He is nature. He is in every cloud, every leaf, and every tree from which a leaf falls in the autumn. He is also the moon, the sun, the void of space and the very DNA makes up my body. Maybe that is why the bible tells us he made us in his image. But whatever, he is life itself. Does anyone want to walk away from that?

How Can I praise you?

I sing hymns of love and grace and declare undying love for you.
Although I sing, I never feel as if I have praised enough, no matter
what I say or do.
I tell the world of your wondrous love but talk is cheap and echoes only
a fleeting second.
The distance between us is so great that I feel I cannot reach you when
I am beckoned.

Oh Lord, I am so grateful that your long arms are reaching for me.
For if they did not it would be a fearful life for I would know not where
I'd be.
I could preach and tell the world about my Lord who holds my soul
within his arms.
But, as I have said, "talk is cheap," and sometimes even meaningless.

I try to express to those around me how much you comfort me when I
am in distress.
I praise you for you patience and because you help me learn from
living.
Praising you simply is not enough for; just like you I want to be the one
who is giving
I want to give to those who need and those with tears and those who
think you are not there.

Because your love for me is saving my soul, I feel that I need to work
for others.
Singing praises to your holy name is not enough unless it touches the
hearts of my sisters and my brothers.

However I will continue to praise you, thanking you for every day you
have given me.
If I help just one sad person find you how grateful I will be.
I pray I can touch one life in the name of the Lord my God and Jesus,
his only Son.
Then I will humbly praise in silence for my eternity has begun.

My mother always said, "Be careful what you pray for. You may get it." I
have found that when I pray, it is better not to ask for things. The truth is if
I need it, God already knows. Jesus gave us a beautiful model of what prayer
should be. Recite the Lords prayer. It is a prayer of praise and
thanksgiving. It asks only for God to hear it. It reminds us that God is the
source of all life. With that in mind, I have written this Thanksgiving
Prayer.

Thanksgiving Prayer

Dear Lord and Heavenly Father I pray to you each day.
As I pray the only thing I find I can of to say
Is, Thank you, Lord for skies, be they blue or gray.

Thank you for the clouds that form high in the skies.
I praise you that they are like music a wonder to my eyes.
Thank you Lord for you have sent all the clear summer nights.
I gratefully admire the darkness and its lesser lights.

Thank you for the moon and the stars each night as they shine and glimmer.
I am even in awe of how the sun diminishes as it grows dimmer.
Thank you Lord for you have made the blossoms that bloom in the spring.
I praise you for the wondrous sound I hear from the birds that sing.

They are singing their own hymns for they praise I think they you as I do.
Springtime, winter, summer and autumn are all gifts from you.
Each has a beauty which defines it in its own special way.
I thank you for all of my yesterdays and also for today.

You have given me life Dear Heavenly Father who watches over me always.
This is why I fear not tomorrow but look up with a faith allowing me to live out my days.
Thank you, my Lord for you have given me eyes with which to see
Not only what is but what can also come to be.

Your love has been my source of love which I want to share with others.
I thank you that you have taught me to love my sisters and brothers.
Thank you Lord. I know not how I can ever try to repay
Yet, I will live as best I can for you each and every day.

Remember that story about Aladdin? He rubbed a lamp and out came a Gene who said he could have three wishes. My grandchildren really loved the Disney movie about that. Aladdin wanted to become a Prince so he could marry the beautiful Princess. His wishes lead him on an adventure he did not ask for. Our prayers are like that. I have already mention that my mother had a saying she loved to use. "Be careful what you wish for, you may get it." Well, OK so I changed it a little bit but it still means the same thing.

I have asked myself many times, "Why not simply ask God to heal my heart and I would no longer need so much medicine?" He answers me. If I ask for worldly gifts, good health, treasures, lots of money. They will only last for a while. If I ask for Heavenly gifts they are forever. That, my friends means eternity. What good would money do in Heaven? If I begin to love it too much it may block my way. I wrote the following because I think the Lords Prayer is beautiful and comforting.

He Taught Us How to Prayer

Jesus gave us a guideline to follow when we pray.
We should first remember to bow our head and then begin to say,

"Our Father, which art in Heaven"

Acknowledge him as our Lord, God and Creator
Someone who is with us now and who we know will be with us later.

"Hallowed be thy name"

Praise the Lord with all thy heart and all thy soul and thy entire mind.
Praise him with all the spiritual energy that within your heart you can find.

"Thy kingdom come, thy will be done on Earth as it is in Heaven"

We pray for a seat in his Heavenly kingdom.
That is why we ask for it to come.
We also ask that God's will be done.
This is made possible because he gave his son.

"Give us this day our daily bread."

Ask yourself this. If you ask for materialistic food will tomorrow again bring hunger?
You will wake up again one day older and wishing you felt younger.

"Forgive us our debts as we forgive our debtors."

This, my friend is the true bread of God our love for his only Son.
Once we learn to forgive and love our Spiritual war is all but won.

"Lead us not into temptation but deliver us from evil"

When we feel the need to do something wrong
Let us pray to God or sing a spiritual song.

For the temptations are great and our soul is weak.
And when the evil doer would lead us astray it is unto the Lord we
need to speak.

"For yours is the Kingdom and the Power and the Glory"

Once again his prayer leads back to acknowledging him,
Praising him and asking for spiritual bread from which all good deeds
do stem.

"Forever, Amen!"

He did not ask us to pray for things of this world because he knows
they soon pass away.
He instructed us to ask for spiritual strength to face each day.
It is for these things he asks us to pray.

I did some math and though I never gave a thought of just how many days I
have lived I find that I have existed on this earth 22,477 days. Now that
makes me feel old. I don't even want to count the seconds. One thing I know
about life is that we should live each and every day for all its worth.
Yesterday is past, tomorrow may never come. That leaves us with today.
That is why it is called the present. Every one of those days I have lived have
been a present from God. I only want to thank him and praise him for each
of them.

What means this Thing called Time?

My mind dwells upon Yesterday for then it was today.
Alas yesterday is no longer today for time has moved it out of the way.
Yesterday brings memories of something in my past
For it was always doomed that yesterday should never ever last.

But in the greater scheme of history God has worked his will.
Out of the void left by yesterday came a new day that void to fill.
For when yesterday relinquished its title of today
It made room for a replacement of what was yesterday.

Now today is here for a short time given by God for us to live.
Is today not a good time for us to love others and for us to give?
For, oh too soon today you see will become yesterday
For this day that we now call today was never really meant to stay

And tomorrow will fill the void left by today and become a brand new
day
As today, just as yesterday reluctantly relinquishes its place.
Tomorrow will then become a new day another today for us to face
And so forth the next day and then the next each a part of life's hectic
race.

Yes, all of my yesterdays have gone away.
They have left me feeling older, my hair turning gray
But I care not that the days, months and years pass so quickly by.
I care not because each new day I awaken with a sigh.
Today is here and today is now.

Yesterday is a memory that stays with me somehow.
I pray to God only that I have learned from yesterday.
I pray that I have grown stronger to live a better today.
Just as God gave me yesterday and blessed me with the day before

He gave me love and forgiveness, I can ask for nothing more.
Don't count the days, my friend for it is better that we should live
them.
Let us sing praises to God and live all your today's giving ourselves to
him.

There have been many times when I felt alone. I felt this in spite of the love
of my wife and children as well as my friends, I was facing an emptiness
which ate at my very soul. I look back on those times now and realize that
my Lord was always there and calling but I did not hear. One wonderful
day, I recognized his voice and his comfort helps me over even the hardest of
times.

I walked the Path I chose

I walked the path I chose or at least I thought I did.
I trudged along through the dark and cold.
I found that as down the path I tread
I felt more lost, confused and old.

One day to my great joy I saw him walking with me.
I wondered why it was that before I did not see
That it was the Son of God who walked with me.

Had he just joined me in my walk?
Had he simply come on that day to talk?
Had he been with me all along?
But I could not hear his heavenly song?

Now that I see him walking by my side
I find that from his glorious love I cannot and will not hide.
Nor do I want to run away from such pure and wonderful love.
For Jesus came to me from God above

He came to show me what true love can do.
He is here for me and also for you.
He once hung on the cross high above the crowd.
As the sky was darkened the thunder rumbled loud.

When the light was once again restored
The people mourned the death of our Lord.
But death had not enough power to create an end.
For it was for this purpose his son God did send.

He defeated death to mark the way
And that is why he walks with me each day.
As my hand reached to accept his hand
I realized that without him I could not stand.

He gently guided me in Heavens direction.
Life has many paths for our selection.
But now I know that if I go the wrong way
God's Son, Jesus Christ will simply say,
"Watch thy step for I will not let you fall."
When he comes to you I pray you will hear his call.

We all want salvation. We all want eternal life. We all want blessings from our Heavenly Father. Notice the word want keeps coming up here? We want but do we give? Can we not better ourselves if we can be a gentle reminder of God's love to the whole world by living his word and following his way?

Self-esteem!

Self-esteem, self improvement, self preservation
Hold on a second, what is wrong with this situation?
Self, self, self... it goes on and on
And it will lead to a point where the ability to love others is gone.
Do we spend too much time protecting ourselves from the world where we live?
Do we not realize that safety has a price of its own to pay, for if we care not then we do not give?
Self-esteem comes from what we accomplish in life.
It is not born on the winds of avoiding hurts and strife.
Self improvement is a product of being a friend of those in need
And self preservation is nothing more, my dear friends than our salvation.
Let us take self out of the equation and dwell on why we are here.
It is because our Master created us and, yes he holds us dear.
His love makes it possible for me to love myself but that's not all.
We gain nothing if we do not love others as ourselves and do not meet Gods call.
If we would feel truly good about ourselves we must first put our lives into Gods hands.
We must proclaim his love in humble forgiveness for it is this by which he stands.
God loves us so we can love others.
Even those who don't know him are our sisters and brothers
And if we do not witness how will they ever know?
Our witness can be quiet friendship which we spread as we go
From place to place and town to town.
We can quietly live by his love and they will see without our making a sound.
I will simply trust in God for my salvation.
I will praise him in work and deed even if in tribulation.
For at the end of my journey I know he will embrace me.
I'll meet him in his home beyond the sky where we will spend eternity.
For now, I simply live as best as I can for my Lord.
I will live his plan for us all. This plan will speak louder than words.

It's kind of funny. I may start out simply reflecting upon the beauty all around me. It could be the moon, the sun. It could be trees in autumn or spring flowers blooming. I always end up praising God and thanking him for his wondrous love. There is no escaping it. All that is, is a reflection of our creator.

Moonshine

I have watched the moon rise over the sea
I have watched the light sprinkle for us to see.
The light bounces off the caps of the waves as they flow.
Creating the appearance of moving mountains topped with snow.

The moons sole purpose is not to create such a sight.
For it is an instrument to replace darkness with light
I contemplate the fact that moonlight bouncing off the sea in my direction
Is not the moons own light but simply a reflection.

That light is created by sun which bounces off the moon toward my eye.
I can see it fully visible at times and sometimes hidden by the clouds in the sky.
Then there are times when the moon sheds no light,
It hides behind the earths shadow completely out of sight.

Even when the moon is darkened it still affects the tides.
Its pull creates the sound of the waves as the ocean rides.
The ocean dances in the darkness sometimes enhanced by the light.
This creates a beautiful and glorious sight.

The sun and the moon are like father and son.
The moon is a reminder that we still have the sun.
This is what Jesus is like to you and to me.
He came reflecting Gods love that we may all see

"See what?" you may ask. God's love which eternally will be.
Jesus said, "no one comes to the Father except through me.

I used the argument which the next poem is based on when I was a salesman with a local radio station. Advertisers were moving more and more to TV. They would say a picture is worth a thousand words. I beg to differ.

Paint with Words

A picture paints a thousand words
At least that's what they say.
I say a picture cannot catch the waves that surge
But if thou give me a thousand words, I'll paint a more beautiful
picture any day.

I can describe the waves flowing too and fro or the beauty of the sky.
I can tell you how I picture them and explain to you just why.
I can describe the soft pink dogwood blossom as it slowly forms in
spring.
I can catch the essence of the autumn air when the crickets no longer
sing.

A thousand words cannot completely describe the beauty of Gods
creation
But a picture is frozen still in time without movements' revelation.
But as I describe the sun which comes peaking over the eastern horizon

You can simply close your eyes and allow yourself to imagine.
The thousand words is a beginning upon which you can build upon.
You can start from there and see the stars, the planets and the son.
There is a wonderful joy in simply letting your mind fill in the blanks.

It can bring back childhood fishing trips with Dad, standing on river
banks.
This is why I am driven to write about life's cares and joys.
For my writings are meant to spur the minds of little girls and boys.
I also write for men and women of all ages who will indulge themselves
to try.
They can see the wonder of life in all it's fullness as if watching dreams
go by.

I think we have all been too quick to speak out in anger when hurt by
another. I know I have. Words cannot be taken back. You can apologize
and should do so when you find that you have let negative emotions drive you
to say things too quickly. However, those words have been spoken and will
always resound themselves. Pray for grace and God can help us all
overcome.

Speak not in Haste!

Do not let yourself speak in anger or resentment that may you feel
For those words are clouded with these emotions.
These words make wounds that may not heal.
Think about what you say and save the dire commotion.

Consider why you feel these things and diligently search your heart.
If you take the time to search your heart you may choose your words
with care.
You may choose to speak with forgiveness, a more creative start.
Anger clouds your judgment and thus your words will be unfair.

Love will be the catapult which will help you rise above
You can lift over the need for angry words and resentment.
And search within your heart and soul for capacity to love.
If you do this you will save your self the agony and replace it with
contentment.

Your soul will sing praises to his holy name
And you will commune with him with peaceful mind.
If love and forgiveness is what you give, you will surely receive the
same.
Love breeds love forgiveness and brotherhood and they are the tides
that bind.

It is better to live and love and to quickly to forgive
It is better not to carry the heavy burden of hate.
For this burden will become heavier for you with every day you live.
Apologize and make amends with your brother or sister before it is too
late.

Think on Things Spiritual
Finally, brothers, whatever is true,
Whatever is noble, whatever is right
Whatever is pure, whatever is lovely
Whatever is admirable. If anything is excellent
Or praiseworthy
Think about these things.
Whatever you have learned or received
Or heard from me, or seen in me...
Put these things into practice.
And God of peace will be with you!
Philippians 4:8, 9

Think on Things Spiritual

All things are created by the one true living force.
He made the sun and moon and the Earth
Our union with him is a marriage from which we cannot divorce.
If we spend our life and dwell on the beauty of his great creation
This becomes the first step toward the greatest of all revelation.

If we dwell on the God's goodness and the love of his only son
We will live on in his Heavenly Kingdom when our earthly life is done.
Think on things that are positive and the beauty all around.
Think about the love of God and peace of mind is easily found.

Do not let yourself dwell on the disappointments of life
Praise God with all your heart and give yourself to his only son.
He will give you strength to deal trials and strife
You will find the wonder of life through his love will have just begun!

The Healing Power of God!

A few years ago I met a lady who was trying to help me but I could not make her understand that I was not going to beg God to heal me of my heart condition. She did not understand why. This is written to explain to you what I truly believe I am lead by God to write.

Jesus performed many miracles and although the Scribes and Pharisees tried to stop him those miracles caused the multitudes to adore him. He calmed the sea. He walked on water and healed the sick. He even brought one man back from the dead and the multitudes worshipped him.

Some said he was a profit. Others said he was the Christ. All loved him as long as he kept the miracles coming. He even changed water into wine.

When Jesus went through the temple and overturned the money changers tables crying, "You have turned my fathers' house into a den of thieves." Things changed.

Now he was telling the multitudes to change their ways and they did not want this. The same people who had previously worshipped him now condemned him. He hung on that cross and performed one more miracle, although not everyone witnessed this one. Thomas did not believe it was Jesus until he saw the marks they had placed on his body.

You may ask why this affects me in the way it does and I can only tell you that I would rather believe out of faith than proof. This was what I was trying to tell this lady. Every time I would cry out to be healed the Holy Spirit interceded. It was praying for my soul and spirit. This is in the scripture, "It is appointed once for every man to die." Shall I pray God will erase this from the Good Book?

Eternal life in a place of peace sounds better and better to me the older I get. Therefore I can only allow the spirit to pray for me. When I pray I praise God. I know not what the future holds but I know who holds the future and that is comfort enough for me. If I have an affliction to bear than so be it. Jesus took on an awful affliction for us.

This is why my prayers are as they are. This is why I realize that all things work for the good of those who love the Lord. All things.... Even heart attacks. Trust in Jesus and give your heart to God the father, God the son and God the Holy Ghost and you will overcome everything, even death.

I was reading from Corinthians as the Apostle Paul wrote of boasting. It was not himself he was boasting about but God's wondrous love. He also spoke of meekness and great humility. All these can find a place in the hearts of those who love the Lord.

"To keep me from becoming conceited because of these surpassingly great revelations, there was given me a thorn in my flesh, a messenger of Satan to torment me. 2 Cor. 12

Is It a Sin for Me?

Is it a sin for me to lower myself in order to rise up a brother?
Is it not an act of love from God that makes me do no other?

I am not boasting when I speak of faith which overcomes my very
weakness.
For if I boast I boast of Gods' great power and pray to him in
meekness.

Because I love my Lord so much I cannot help but boast.
It is not of me that proclaim these wonders but to the Lord of hosts.

God so loved the world that he gave his only Son.
He lived and loved and healed and than bore our sins before his
Earthly job was done.

Although he accomplished all he came to Earth to do he did not stop at
this.
He has sent the Holy Spirit to lift us up with a glorious kiss.

The spirit drives me to boast of his amazing love and power.
Though I, myself feel weak and frail he guides me through each hour.

He guides me by the Spirit toward Heavens Holy Shore.
From there, I will know the cares of this life no more.

I will see him face to face and I will embrace him with great passion.
I will praise him for eternity for his great love, wisdom and
compassion.

Jesus once said, "Except ye be as little children you cannot enter the
Kingdom of Heaven.

Through the Eyes of a Child!

It warms your heart when the baby first makes eye contact.
He is becoming aware of the world around.
Any parent knows of the wonderful impact
Of his smile when he looks or responds to your voices sound.

The child will grow older and his world will expand.
He will watch flowers in bloom and examine the sky.

You have watched as he first learns to crawl and then stand.
If you watch closely you can see his mind asking questions like why.

Why are the skies so blue with wondrous clouds of white?
He witnesses his first spring, summer, winter and fall.
He is enthralled by the beauty of the butterfly's flight.
His mind is inundated by the wonder of it all.

What is sad is that like us, he will grow to be old.
He will have little time to admire the Gods' wonderful creation.
His childhood fantasies will die and grow cold
And he will become skeptical and sometimes not prone to elation.

Let us take a trip into yesteryear if we dare.
Let's visit our past and remember the innocence.
Let us find our long dormant childhood eyes that stare
And wonder about the miracles that set just beyond the next fence.

Can we go back to our childhood when our faith was so pure?
Can we relish in the wonderful gift of Gods' love?
Do we have the courage to open that magical door?
And walk into our past, bring it to the future and move above?

We can lift ourselves out of our world of worry
And love as a child of God who has learned the secret.
We wait upon the Lord and live not in a hurry
But rather take time to enjoy every moment with no time for regret.

We are children of God and his arms are loving and strong.
If we reach for him as a child reaches for his mother
His immaculate love will carry us along.
He will teach us to love our sister and brother.

That is why he sent us his son. That is why Jesus was born
To take us all back to the innocence of our childhood.
To take us to a time when we did not question or scorn.
Embrace him like the child that we are and we will learn what is
righteous and good.

It is a real challenge to take God's word and make a poem out of it. I do
hope I did not take anything away from the meaning. This poem was
inspired by God and I truly believe that in writing it I actually was forced to
capture the true meaning of Gods word. I hope you enjoy it.

Celebrate the Birth of Christ

John the Baptist came preaching and saying "Repent for the Kingdom
is at hand.
For the only Son of God is coming to lift your sins away."
John preached the word to all who heard from east to west throughout
the land.
John baptized with water but soon, he said "Another comes to whom I
will gladly pray."

I am not worthy to bear the shoes of the mighty one who comes next to
you.
He is much mightier than I and will baptize with fire and with the Holy
Ghost of God.
When Jesus came to be baptized John proclaimed, "This I am not
worthy to do."
Jesus answered "Suffer it to be so now: for this we must fulfill for it is
prophesied."

Therefore John did baptize him and as Jesus came out of the waters,
straightway
The heavens were opened and he saw the spirit descending like a dove.
Then heard them all the voice of God on this wondrous and glorious
day.
"This," he said, "is my beloved Son, in whom I am well pleased and
love.

This my Brothers and Sisters is why we celebrate
Jesus came to save our souls and call us away from sin.
He came to make our blind eyes see before it was too late.
And now we pray to God the father and serve him once again.

Merry Christmas!

Someone sent me an email that is quoted like this. "Life is like a roll
of toilet paper. The closer you get to the end the quicker it goes." Well I
laughed at the irony and then I began to consider this. Life is just like that.
You could also liken it to a bar of soap.

Soap on a String!

Life is like soap on a string which hangs in my shower stall.
Each day I use a little soap to clean myself with the lather that it will lend.
I've been using it for a while and I see it is getting rather small.
Soon there will be nothing left but the string for the soap has come to its end.

This is not a bad way to look at life for if I can be like that soap which gives.
I can give a little of myself and help others see Gods holy light.
I can be a source of refreshing cleanliness and renewal as my brother lives.
I can share my love, my faith and share with others some of Christ's insight.

In this way when like that bar of soap my life I have already given
I will have the honor of knowing that I have touched the lives all around.
Someone will know Gods love through me and they will see their sins forgiven.
Though the string will hang empty, the soap of Gods love is proven to be profound

Perhaps my brother will leave the string hang there as a tribute to my life.
Perhaps the string will be there to console whenever he felt he has lost a friend.
It may be reason enough for him to live through happiness as well as strife.
He will see the string and know that I am with God, the soap maker who has no end.

I noticed one of those billboards that have been posted around our area.
They have said things like, "Don't make me come down there," signed God.
Or "For God so loved the world that he did not send a committee." Another said "CH__RCH! What is missing, U. R."
The one I really like is, "My way is the Highway." That prompted the following poem.

My Way!

You have heard people say it many times I am sure.
It may be your boss or your mother or dad.
It makes us conform to whatever life has in store.
Well, I can only say that is really too bad.

"My way or the highway," they sternly proclaim.
This means that they think there is no other way.
However, this closes doors on relationships and that is a shame.
Our Heavenly Father has something better to say.

"My way is the high way," he says in a powerful voice.
If we follow his way it will lead to everlasting life with our Lord.
So, you see my dear friend it is a matter of choice.
Do we follow his way and live by his word?

The alternative is a life that is lived without faith hope and love.
If we take the high road we will be in his presence always.
Our sins will be forgiven and our souls lifted above.
We will live our lives held securely in his mighty arms.

Let's take the "High way!"

Many people are afraid to truly love. Love, they think exposes them to hurt so they shield themselves from this uncertain thing called love. They shield themselves from the truest source of happiness. It may be that I have already written about this in this very book. In face, I think I have but I do not think you can voice enough the importance of stepping out in faith and daring to love at any cost.

Emptiness is a void we can fill!

If you look at your life as empty and old
It is possible it is so because you do not dare
To fill the emptiness with someone to hold
Someone who has the power to make you care.

If you look at your life as an empty page
It is a page begging for you to fill in the blank
It is possible that you have an internal war to wage.
A war between you and yourself and if you win you will have your own
self to thank.

Emptiness is a lack of love freely given which inspires love in return.
It is true you will become vulnerable and there could be heartache.
What you need to ask is this, "Does my heart not now burn?"
The answer my friend is 'this is a chance you must take.'

To love is to open your heart and your soul to those around.
To love is to allow your own self to tear an emotional wall down.
Love will allow you to bask in the wonderful sound
Of songs about caring, joy, sharing where happiness can abound.

Let not yourself dwell in seclusion so lonely and hiding in fear.
It is good to live, love and be happy for there are great treasures to be
had.
Love you sister and brother and that one you hold dear.
Live, love, forgive and fill in the void and take good with the bad.

If you look at your life as empty and old
You are looking past the key to happiness sublime.
Reach for the dear one you love with your arms to enfold.
For true love will not pass away over time.

Tis the Season

Christmas is almost here as I write this. What is sad it the fact that there are those who are embarrassed to say, "Merry Christmas." There are others who claim they are offended by worshipping Christ or God at all. After all, the other religions don't have their worship rituals. Actually, they do. If they worship Mohammad or Buddha, I am not offended. It causes me to wonder why God makes these people so nervous. I can't in all honesty say that we have not brought a lot of it on ourselves. Christmas is commercialized to the point that many people who are quick to call themselves Christians have become more caught up in giving and receiving presents than in the true meaning of the day.

Madeleine Murray O'Hare decided some time back that she was offended by prayers in the school. Then someone said you should not read the bible in school and now there is talk about taking Christmas carols and pageants out of school.

We as Christians have sat quietly and watched with only some grumping and griping. I must admit my first thought was fine. Take it out of school. It is nothing more than empty words if you are not truly talking to God and listening when he answers. We have also been guilty of another shortcoming. We have allowed our faiths in Jesus drive us apart from one another. You know, Jesus once said, "A house divided against itself cannot stand."

Maybe as Christians we need to show each other a little tolerance. Have you ever wondered why there are so many denominations all of whom claim to be 'The church of God?'

While we separate ourselves from one another how can we withstand the bombardment of those who wish to believe in nothing?

I received an email from a friend which is said to be written by Ben Stein. He is not just a quirky actor/comedian. He is a very intelligent attorney. Oh yes, and he is Jewish. I don't care. Here is a little of what he wrote about Christmas.

"I am a Jew and every single one of my ancestors was Jewish. And it does not bother me even a little bit when people call those beautiful lit up, bejeweled trees Christmas Trees. I don't feel threatened. I don't feel discriminated against. That's what they are. Christmas trees!"

He goes on to say the following:

"It doesn't bother me a bit when people say, 'Merry Christmas' to me. I don't think they are slighting me or getting ready to put me in a ghetto. In fact, I kind of like it. It shows that we are all brothers and sisters celebrating this happy time of year."

Mr. Stein goes on to say that he is not bothered or offended by a manger scene on display at a key intersection near his home in Malibu. He feels it is fine with him just as is the Menorah which sets a few yards away.

He makes a wonderful point. As he put it, and I quote:

I don't like getting pushed around for being a Jew, and I don't think Christians like getting pushed around for being Christians. I think people who believe in God are sick and tired of getting pushed around, period."

There are those who ask if there were a God how he could let catastrophic events like hurricane Katrina happen When Anne Graham, Billy Graham's daughter was asked she had this to say.

"I believe God is deeply saddened by this, just as we are, but for years we've been telling God to get out of our schools, to get out of our government and to get out of our lives and being the gentleman he is, I believe he has calmly backed out."

I think it started with Madeleine Murray O'Hare just as Ben Stein does. I believe that Dr. Benjamin Spock added to the chaos that we find ourselves tolerating when he said we should not spank our children when they misbehave because we might hurt them psychologically. Did you know his son committed suicide?

The bottom line is simple. Why can we not become as brothers and sisters? All of us! I believe what I believe. I will give you the right to believe what you believe without hating you in any way. If we all did this there would be no terrorists. There would be no crime and there would be a much happier life for all of us.

I believe in Jesus Christ, God's only son. I share my faith with Mr. Stein. He may not know Jesus but he knows the father. His writing proves. Jesus once said, "I am the word of God." He also was quick to say, "The word is written on the heart of many without their even knowing it." I believe in him enough to trust his words. Love thy neighbor as thyself.

He did warn of the things which we are now experiencing. He said there would be a falling away from the truth. He told us we would be hated for his name sake. Did he cause it? I don't think so. Much of it is our own doing. Much of it is others desire to hate. Satan can be a sneaky devil. One of his greatest accomplishments was making so many people think he didn't really exist. Now has many thinking God doesn't really exist.

It does make me want to search my soul and be a better follower. Keep in mind that Jesus was not born on December 25th... The early Christians found it easy to worship on the sly because the other option was the people in charge at that time would crucify them if they worshipped on his true birthday. This has been going on for more than two-thousand years. Isn't it ironic that after all this time we have not really changed much in status?

Let us all put our differences aside and proudly proclaim, "Merry CHRISTmas, with the emphasis on Christ. It's his birthday. Let's give him the best present of them all. Let us give him our hearts and souls.

God Bless you one and all!

Some of the most beautiful scriptures in the bible are the Psalms. I like the 23rd. Psalms in particular. Though I could never write such beautiful writings as these, this is one of my Psalms, praising the Lord.

Come out of the Cold

The wind is chilled with flakes of snow falling.
My fingers feel frost bitten from the blustery cold.
Over the sound of the wintry wind I hear someone calling,
"Press on, my child, press on. Be faithful and bold."

"I have promised that you will one day be with me.
You will never feel the cold or pain for you will be set free.
You will know only great joy and hear music that soothes the ear.
For you are my child, one who I truly hold dear."

"Press on through the cold winter's night.
Press on through the summers burning heat.
Know that I am aware of your plight.
There is someone in the glory of Heaven I want you to meet."

The voice is sweet even as it traverses across the cold winter air.
It is the voice of my Savior who leads me to go on.
He knows my joys, my fears as well as heartaches and is willing to care.
In him I find faith to pursuit my dreams for he is my sun.

I will warm my hands with the fire sent from God's Holy Spirit.
When he calls to me I will acknowledge his glory and listen in silence.
His words give great knowledge; I have only to listen that I might hear
it.
For I know that one day I will see Christ coming in great glory and
radiance.

When he comes to harvest all who have not lost faith in the Master
He will lift us up to be with him for eternity in God's wonderful
kingdom.
He will come to save us from the Earths great disaster.
We will live in harmony with him in wonderful freedom.

"Be still, and know that I am God."
Thus saith the Lord.

I thought I would experiment a little as I wrote the next piece. I
wanted to say it quickly and be absolute about my faith. We often do not
allow ourselves the most wonderful comforts which are gifts from God. Let
us look to him for peace of mind.

If I but have the Courage to Live

It is easy to simply allow one self to exist
But it takes faith to live life to its fullest and persist.

It is easy to reason why I cannot try
But with faith I can reach up and touch the sky.

It is simple to sit and resent the blessings shared by others.
But with true Christian love we can share it with sisters and brothers.

How many times have we found ourselves crying?
We say that life is unfair as we sit there sighing.

When God's voice calls us do we simply not hear?
In our deafness do we not acknowledge his love so dear?

Why do we punish ourselves as we do?
Why do we not allow ourselves to be true?

True to ourselves and true to our Lord.
True to his calling, living true to his word.

We can have happiness that money cannot buy.
We must search for it in our hearts and it will not die.

Listen to the melody of the voice of our Lord and our Master.
The beauty we will hear is not cancelled out by any disaster.

For, no matter what life on this Earth may hold in store.
It will mean nothing when we enter through Heavens Golden door.

Trust in God and know you are not alone, ever.
Trust in God and in his love which will stay with you forever.

I was watching TV and another of those wonderful ads about a 'one time only' sale came on. I was feeling kind of whimsical and decided to have some fun. After all, who do they think they are fooling? There have been so many 'one time only' sales that I have lost count. How can one lose count of something that only ever uses the number one? Do you see where I am going with this yet? Read the following poem. It is meant to make you chuckle but you may also find yourself wondering, too.

The more than one time Sale!

"Buy now," they proclaim. "Save while supplies last."
They tell you to come now for the products are going fast.

"This is a one time sale," they loudly shout.
"At these wonderful prices we will soon be sold out."

When we run to the store we find that the dozen or so items are sold.
However there are other items to purchase at great savings, we are
told.

We went for that fantastic comfortable bed to sleep on.
But when we got there we found that alas they are gone.

However before we can walk out of the store
That has placed other items on sale that usually cost more.

"Buy it now," they promise "and you will save and save a lot."
I did not need a new phone with three hand pieces but that's what I
got.

Because I took advantage of this one time only sale I find that I have
spent.
Now I am wondering where it is that my money has went.

Not to worry, though my friend if you missed yesterdays one time sale.
Tomorrow will bring another 'one time' sale. At least that is their tale.

It gives one a reason to pause and wonder on the one hand,
What part of one do they not understand?

For yesterdays sale was the only one while supplies last as they tell.
Today's one time sale has more gadgets to sell.

Now do your math, my friend and you will agree
That one plus one equals two and one more will make three.

Yet they are intent on telling you that each one is the last.
Be careful for if you keep running for savings your money won't last.

This is one more poem I wrote during the Christmas holidays. We are living
in a time when some do not wish to celebrate Christmas. I believe I have
already mentioned that but I will say it again. They fear that in doing so we
will offend others. This is not new to our Lord. They hung him on a cross

because his words offended some who were made blind. Let us not be made blind. Let us worship our Master and know his love always.

His Birth, Life and Death, all Gifts to Us!

He left his throne and came to Earth.
A stable was his place of birth.

He gave himself to his master and to us all.
His life on Earth started as a baby small.

He lived, he loved and he healed the sick and lame.
With his wondrous love he cast away our blame.

When Christ was born they sang to him in praise.
They were amazed at his knowledge in the early days.

As he grew there were those who resented our Lord.
They could not accept the living Word.

They plotted a way to put him to death
How their hearts sank when with his dying breath.

Jesus cried out, "Father forgive them for they know not what they do."
Even the pain would not erase his forgiveness for me and for you.

He left the throne and came to Earth.
A stable was his place of birth.

His death was not a symbol of our loss.
It was for us that he hung there upon the cross.

We celebrate Christmas to recognize his birth.
We celebrate Easter to praise his rebirth.

Because he defeated death he has paved the way.
We will follow him on that final day.

Then we will spend eternity in Heaven above.
We have this hope because of his great love.

He left the throne and came to Earth
We praise our lord…, we praise his birth.

Have you ever had the feeling that the true meaning of Christmas gets lost in all our celebrating. It is good to celebrate Christmas but let us be aware of why we celebrate. That celebration should go on all year long. We should give of ourselves every day and we should know that we do this because Christ first gave his life for us.
Celebrate CHRISTmas but celebrate it because Jesus Christ was born.

It is not a One Day Event!

We celebrate the birth of Christ each December 25th.
We spend the months leading up to it shopping till we are stiff.

Christmas is more that presents and turkey and cranberry relish.
If we think of it as no more than that we are truly foolish.

Christmas is when we celebrate the birth of our salvation.
Jesus came into the world to fulfill God's wondrous creation.

He lived to give, he gave his life and he gave us eternal life.
He lived his life to fulfill the fathers wish and endured all the strife.

He did all this because of eternal love for those who had gone astray.
So when you awaken from your sleep on this most wonderful day

Remember that God so loved the world that he gave his son to save the lost.
Are we willing to take the time to do his will no matter what the cost?

We celebrate the birth of Christ each December 25[th.] each year.
However let us celebrate it everyday for he is always near.

Trust in God and thank him as we celebrate our Saviors birth.
He lived, he loved and he gave his life to bring peace and good will on Earth.

We look back at youthful days and find that we did not accomplish the wonders we set out to fulfill. We look back and see why our world is in turmoil. It starts with each of us. We grow older and wiser but we truly do not have the energy we once had to try to make a difference. The best we can do is encourage our children to make life a better experience for them and those they meet.

Oh to Regain my wasted Youth!

When I was a young man I thought I had all the answers.
Now I know I only thought I did as my empty words stepped to and fro
like dancers.

I look back now and see myself as a young man who was head strong
and cock sure.
I realize that my answers were flawed even though my hopes were
pure.

I pray to God and ask why I was so long in learning and so quickly
growing old?
His answer is simple. "You were young and foolish and that is why you
felt so bold"

I also ask the Lord if my children will be wiser before they grow old
and gray.
His answer, "They must learn from experience as they live out each
and every day."

It seems that youth comes with bliss and that is a blinding light.
As we grow older we find the bliss will not stand through darkened
night.

Each generation must learn for itself what their elders have learned
before.
Nobody knows until they have experience it what life has in store.

The young would change the world and make it a better place.
Somehow the odds are greater that they only learn by the troubles they
must face.

This is why we must remind them now that God is holding their hand.
He loves us all. He cares for us and our troubles he will understand.

I have tried to tell people what I believe is a secret to faith which
drives the soul. It is hard to put it into words and I am sure it is hard to
understand. When I was a child my parents took us to a church which
taught that if you ask anything and have faith, God will give it to you. I have
found this is not so. God knows what I do not know. That being, what I need
and what will save my eternal soul. Think about it friend. He knows my
every thought even before I do and he knows my every need even better than
I do. Who am I to make demands of the very one who gives me ever breath?
I simply turn on my spiritual radio, tune it to station JESUS and listen. Then

I try to put it into works. Not to save myself for I cannot do this. The wonderful news is he is doing it for me. That is why I work for the Lord. His love nourishes my soul and causes me to love in return.

My Fairy GOD Father?

He is God, my creator. He carries my heavy load.
He walks beside me hand in hand as I travel down life's long and lonely road.

He has not touched my body to heal or ease whatever ails
But he is always there to touch my soul with healing that never fails.

I ask no fantastic miracles of my Lord in Jesus' name.
I know that if he wills it, he could heal the sick and lame.

I do not ask much of him for I realize he knows my needs.
I simply come to him in prayer and draw strength to perform good deeds.

I realize that words are useless when I pray to God above.
I simply sit quietly and listen as he speaks with eternal love.

He gives me all I need to live my life in faith in his holy name.
For with this faith I can endure all things, that's why I can proclaim,

He is my lord and Savior; it is his strength that drives my soul.
I am his child and I love to serve for indeed that is my role.

If you find there comes a day that life seems hard for you to endure.
Take your troubles to the Lord for his love is strong and sure.

Try praying silently and without words, simply seeking out his voice.
Then when he gives you his knowledge to boost your faith simply make the eternal choice.

As I wrote the following poem we had not had a snow yet here. I couldn't shovel it anymore but I can still remember being mesmerized by the snowflakes each one of which never seemed to be in a hurry but lazily and gently proceeded to a spot on the ground. As flake fell upon flake the ground was soon white and pure. These memories are what inspired the poem.

What is Life?

Snowflakes lazily floating in the winter air,
Flitting here and there seemingly without a care.

They search for a place where they can lay themselves down
And as they do, they will transform the ground.

They will also cover the nakedness of the trees.
The snowflakes find themselves directed there by the winter's breeze.

It is so much as if someone planned the falling of the snows.
The flakes are not falling but are directed by the crisp wind that blows.

All of life is like that; the spring, summer, winter and fall.
Someone carefully engineered them, one and all.

Someone who knew what would come from his labor of love.
It was he who created the rain, the beasts of the forest and the dove.

The next time you find yourself mesmerized by the snow so white
Look toward the Heavens and proclaim with great delight,

"God I praise you for you have given life for me to live.
Now I will pray you give me faith so that I may give.

Help me give to the poor, to the needy to the downtrodden and sad.
Let me give with a heart that takes great delight and is glad.

For you have first given to me what're I may need.
Give me the will to pass these on by kind word and good deeds.

The Days End

As the peaceful sunset ends another day
It passes on for it knows it cannot stay.

Let not your heart become burdened with regret.

When it has run its given course it not something you forget.

Today ends its run as today but is reborn as yesterday.
It joins the yesterdays, each one which started as a today.

This is how our Earthly lives are laid out.
We live, worship God. His glory we shout.

Just after the sunset when the darkness falls
Our spirit hears the Master when he calls.

He proclaims you are no longer today
For I have another part for you to play.

Now you watch over your loved ones from Heaven above.
They will always know your undying love.

So if you lose a loved one do not suffer in misery
For you have more than just their memory.

You know they are held lovingly in God's arms, eternally strong.
Have faith for you will be with them before very long.

Each day becomes a yesterday and each year is preceded by another.
We do not die but simply pass on to a place where we share joy with
our sister and brother.

Trust in God and know his love for he will lead you through the night.
Know him and know his son who will lead you till the day comes when
you too, take flight.

How we often reflect upon our childhood years which passed so fast.
We may even find ourselves asking God why they could not last.

Our childhood has passed away and we find we have grown up.
One day we will pass on with our Lord to his Kingdom where we will
sup.

So care not what each day may bring
For in your heart and soul you may sing.

Joy to the world, to Lord I have come and here I stay.
A place where there is no night or day.

A place of wonder and a place of joy and glee.
A place where I will gladly live for eternity.

"I Believe," is the name of one of my favorite gospel songs. It speaks to me personally every time I hear it or sing it out myself. It is not the song that fills my heart but an overflow from my heart that makes me sing it. This shares only the title but it tells what I firmly believe in my heart.

I Believe

I believe the sun shines because of his amazing power.
I believe that he stands with me even through my darkest hour.

I believe he speaks with me if I have spiritual ears to hear.
I believe he is the one who gave me the love of those I hold dear.

I also believe that I must give because he first gave to me.
I believe there is a reason for all things that may come to be.

I believe in Jesus Christ because he came from the Father above.
I believe that we have the gift of salvation because of his undying love.

I believe that love like his is like a flower that grows.
I believe it is also brighter than the sun that glows.

I believe that everything we see or hear is a part of He who made us what we are.
I see him in the darkness of night and in the moon and each and every star.

If I do not respond to his everlasting love in faith and repentance I will have turned away from my source of life and lost my claim to innocence.

If believe that God and Jesus Christ are one and the same.
It was by the power of God that Jesus drew upon to heal the lame.

I believe that all my life has been fashioned by his will and might.
It has been because he has opened my eyes that I now have his insight.

I praise not myself for the sight to see or spiritual ears to hear.
I praise my Heavenly Father through Jesus Christ who in my heart I hold dear.

What I sometimes find myself contemplating is my motives for serving God. Is it simply so I will go to Heaven when I die? I really believe that if this is the reason I tarnish my soul with self serving ideas. I truly believe that we all start that way but as years go by our love for our creator is based on the fact that he loved us first. I would like to think when I serve God I do so because he first loved me. My eternal salvation is a gift from God. I couldn't earn it. I shouldn't try. I simply am caught up in his wonderful love and that breeds more love on my part.

From Where Cometh Salvation?

From where cometh my salvation?
How will I know that it is come?
It is not announced like a train pulling into the station.
I have no eyes that see from whence it comes.

If I cannot see where it comes from or when it has arrived
I must conclude that it comes like a thief in the night.
Is it possible that it through life's turmoil has survived?
Only driven by God's wondrous might?

It may be that my Salvation is not yet complete.
It may be that each day I gain a small part.
Maybe each small part is a daily treat
Which bolsters my soul and fulfills my heart.

From where cometh my salvation?
How can I know that it ever will come?
I pray to my Lord and my heart glories in elation.
I praise God from hence my ability to love has come.

What is salvation if it is not total love?
Is it simply a means to immortality?
I believe it is more than a free ticket to Heaven above.
I believe it brings immortality with much greater quality

From where cometh my salvation?
This is a question I should not need to ask.
For it comes from God through his Son and my Lord.
It comes from God's powerful and everlasting word.

Well, as I write the next piece it is the beginning of another year. I have always found that New Years resolutions are easy to make and hard to keep. I wonder why we feel compelled on the first of every year to make promises about our activities in the coming years. The future has not yet come to be. Therefore, how can I with clear conscience promise something that I may or may not do?

No More Resolutions

Every year it is a tradition, one that I believe is made in dilution.
We make a promise to one in all. It is called a New Years Resolution.

This seems to be a waste of time indeed.
For as the new years days ahead proceed

We almost always find ourselves breaking
The New Year's resolution we are undertaking.

So my New Years resolution this year will be
That there are no more resolutions made by me.

Why promise myself I will cut down on eats
Or possibly I will eat much less meats.

These promises are made once a year on this day
And followed by days where our passions sway.

The only problem with this resolution I have made
Is the fact, that the resolution has already been disobeyed.

If indeed I promised myself by resolution
I have already failed to find the solution.

I said no more resolutions but in fact I have already made one.
So I will postpone my resolution until another year has begun.

HAPPY NEW YEAR!

I wrote this as I was watching the Funeral of Gerald R. Ford on the TV set. I could care less if he was a republican, democrat or whatever. He was a calming voice in a time when our nation had gone made with uneasiness. Wars, scandals and unrest caused us to become worried about our nations future. We are fighting those same battles today. Maybe that is one of many reasons why the funeral of President Ford means to much.

Tribute to Gerald R. Ford

Someone once said old presidents never die
They just fade away.
I find this to be a bit of a lie
As I watch his funeral service today.

It is true that the presidency of Gerald Ford faded as years went by.
We had forgotten that he was a voice of calm during a time of a great
unrest
But upon his death a spark ignited and I think that I know why.
Only after he passed away are we reminded that he tried to do what
was best.

Our nation goes through trying times and we often go astray.
We often forget what it is that our forefathers dreamed for us all
We think that in this new age we have found a better way.
Only after we have failed do we realize that we can fall.

A voice which calms us in times of trial is a gift from God above.
He was a simple man and never dreamed that he would be one day
The president of the United States but he heard the call and answered
undying in love
Rest in Peace, Mr. President and join the Master in Heaven to stay

There are preachers in churches and on TV and people everywhere
you go who want to know if you are saved? My answer is, "I shall be!" God
is still working and his presence has not been stripped from my mind so I
know he has not given up. He will forgive as long as I can honestly admit I
need it. He will wax me strong and he will guide me. He may tug a little
harder sometimes when he knows I am tempted to go astray but he will not
leave me. I only pray that I will never be foolish enough to leave him.

Yesterday

Yesterday is a dim reflection in my mind.
I see it only in part for much of it is now forgotten
As I desperately search for something to remind
Me of what transpired or things I had begotten.

Try as I may I cannot remember all my yesterdays
For there are too many and they went by too fast.
I know only that I could have lived them better in many ways
And though I would have saved them they could not last.

Why are my yesterdays so important to me?
Why do I not live my life faithfully using what I have learned?
Why do I not make myself as strong in the ways of the Lord as I can
be?

I only know that even the moments I have not recollected
Are kept in a log book in God's Holy Heaven.
It is these things of life upon which I will have reflected
Before I meet my Savior whose number is seven.

It is not important that I remember what happened thirty years ago.
It is more important that what I have learned I can maintain.
For when Jesus comes to gather us with his glorious glow
We will all be asked to search our souls and entertain.

Entertain the notion that although we are not perfect
It is important that we are able to say that we tried.
It is also important that we confess the times when we were derelict.
Upon doing so our entrance into his Kingdom will not be denied.

I think I may have mentioned this before but I will risk saying it
again. Our life in the eyes of God would probably amount to a couple of
seconds. God is for eternity but my physical body grows old and eventually
will wear out. My spirit is a different story. It can live for eternity but only
if I accept my Savior as my Lord and my God.

In a Few Seconds

Now as I hit my golden years I find that I have grown old so fast.
I realize that life has left me with a mixture of memories.
Of days of youth that could not last.

I treasure many of those memories and dread some others.
I experience a feeling of deep exhaustion.
I remember fishing trips with my father and brothers.
I reflect upon the times spent with aunts and uncles and all my
relations.

I simply remember some of them now, for they have already been
called to the sky.
My mother and father are with God today as is my brother I pray.
For one by one my elders have been escorted to the sweet by and by.
I will treasure their memory until my Master says to me, "come, and
do not delay.

I am calling your spirit to your heavenly home.
You will not know sadness for there is no place for it here.
This will be a home from which you never wish to roam.
You will never know worry and never know fear.

You will sup with the Angels and forever live free.
In Heaven there will be no restraints for they are not needed.
True happiness will be yours and once you have seen eternity
You will realize that your Earthly life was short but blessed for my
words you have heeded.

This is my faith. This is what I believe God has in mind for me. Why? I know not. I have not earned his love but he has chosen to love me anyway. I can't explain how is this is possible for he has chosen to forgive, to strengthen and to prepare me for a life that is yet to come. Faith is an interesting thing. If I could prove it to yourself or anybody else, it would not be faith. Jesus once said, "Blessed is he who has not seen and yet believes."

The Spirit Keeps Searching

My body grows old and my hair turns gray.
I get oh so tired by the end of each and every day.

I know that this physical being is slowly wearing out.
It is doomed one day be buried in a box of that there is no doubt.

But my spirit is only restrained by my body right now.
Once the body gives up the ghost the spirit is released somehow.

It will fly to the sky. It will unite with my Lord on Heavens golden
shore.
My spirit will live for eternity. It only needs to pass through Heavens
door.

I know that death will be the last sting of life on this earth.
My body started to age from the moment of my birth.

But my spirit knows no limits and prays only for God's love and care.
My spirit through Christ can go where my body would not dare.

Life is a constant changing. It broadens causing our hearts to expand.
When we have grown enough in the Spirit then the Spirit will surely
stand.

It will stand by the Master and converse with his son.
It will praise God long after my earthly life is done.

I praise God for his love for he has made all that is on the earth.
I praise him for he has shown me the reality of my spirits worth.

So fear not death and fear not the future or what it may bring.
Know that your spirit will stand with our Lord, share praises and sing.

Hey man, I am 61 years old. If regaining my youth was a simple
matter of reversing the numbers I could be 16 again. That is not going to
happen in this world. As we get older we have a tendency to wish for the
'good ole' days. The fact is that no matter how old we get we should be living
for today. I am the father of three. I am a grandfather of five. I have eight
bundles of joy that can bring joy into my heart. Why long for the good ole
days. I am living them.

Where have they gone?

"Where have they gone?" I ask myself for truly I miss them so.
The good times enjoyed in my youth. The ones I used to know.

Did they fade away with my youth and slowly disappear?
Did they become more and more tired with each long passing year?

Why do I not feel like the young man that I once used to know?
Why is it that those happy times could not stay? Why did they have to
go?

In truth if I am still looking for the magic of the wonder days of
yesteryear.
If those are the only memories which my heart can hold close and dear

I have a problem with my heart for it has become farsighted and blind.
You see every day brings more good times which are why the old is left
behind.

Look up and thank the Lord above for every day you live.
Follow him and never miss the chance to share or the opportunity to
give.

God knows that life is full of good times which come with each and
every breath.
He knows the joy of living and he knows the glory of death.

So live for today and keep in mind that tomorrow these will be good
times remembered.
So, live each second, minute, hour and day for they are surely
numbered.

Keep in mind that eternity is waiting just beyond the sky.
When we meet the Master in Heaven we will know the reason why.

Why those days of yesteryear were meant to pass away.
They make more room for more new experiences as we live from day
to day.

I received another email from a friend yesterday. It was a list of
favorite sayings by the immortal Will Rogers. They are cute and comical but
they are also extremely meaningful. I am going to try to use some of them in
a rhyme. Wish me luck!

A Tribute to Will

Will Rogers was a man of words that were comical and meaningful.
They were always anything but boring, hollow or dull.

Here is one of his sayings that if you tried it you would know.
"Never slap a man who's chewing a wad of tobacco."

"Never kick a cow chip on a hot day," was another useful tip.
For one thing it will really smell and it might just make you slip.

Will had this advice for men who like to argue with their wife like
jerks.
"There are two theories to arguing with a woman," he says. "And
neither of them works."

This next piece of advice is good for both husband and wife.
"Never miss a good chance to shut up," he says and that makes a more
peaceful life.

Here is one of my favorites and it applies to us, every one.
"If you find yourself in a hole, stop digging," Better yet, don't start and
you will have won.

Will had this advice about growing older and I find I like to hear it.
"Eventually you will reach a point when you stop lying about your age
and start bragging about it."

"Some people try to turn back their odometers," he said as he smiled
and waved.
"Not me, I want people to know 'why' I look this way. I've traveled a
long way and some of the roads were not paved."

I cannot find words to adequately praise God for his love overcomes
all the cares of this world. I feel sorry for those who do not have this
wonderful joy. Knowing his love which was given to one who truly never
earned it is a greater joy than I can find words to express.

Oh the Joy

Oh how my soul cries out with joy and love so dear.
It rejoices in the sound of Angels singing which I can hear.

It is not with physical ear that I hear the Angels voices.
It is in spirit that I hear the sound of their praises as each Angel
rejoices.

Oh how my soul cries out with love and glee.
It rejoices for the image of God is mine to see.

I did not see God with mortal eye it is blind to his vision.
I see with my soul the love of Jesus Christ who made my salvation his
mission.

Oh how my soul cries out with joy and love so real.
It cries out because of the joy of God's presence which I feel.

My mortal body knows not this wonderful sensation.
The feeling is a gift from the spirit of loving devotion.

Oh how my soul cries with joy and thanksgiving.
It is thankful for the gift given by God's son who lived and is still
living.

He left his thrown and came down from Heaven to show us all the way.
It was the greatest love ever shown and it lives on today.

Oh how my soul cries out in humble confession.
It praises the one who died for all of our transgressions.

He did not have to hang there crying out on that cross.
However had he not, it would have been our greatest loss.

That is why my soul cries out in humility and love.
For the gift from God was the life of his son, Jesus Christ, the Dove

I have a pet cat that I have grown very fond of. She seems to have her
own way of looking at the world but even in her eyes I am compelled to see
the wonders of God's world.

Eyes of a Cat

She has eyes that see in darkness and she roams about at night.
It does not matter to her that nowhere is found a light.

She looks at things that move about untroubled by darkness all
around.
She becomes a traveler as she hears each cricket's lonely sound.

She has eyes that see in darkness and she roams the night alone.
In great curiosity she searches for treasures as through the night she
will roam.

She seems content to be in the dark and never Secom's to worry.
She knows the darkness is her turf and she never seems to hurry.

She has eyes that see in darkness but she knows soon comes the
morning light.
She knows that the morning sun will announce the end of another
night.

If we believe in Jesus Christ, the Son of the living God above and all
around
We will know that just as the cat understands that the night will end
we will soon hear the trumpets sound.

We have eyes that see in darkness but we search patiently for the light.
We can see the true source of eternal happiness and the true creator of
delight.

Jesus Christ will come through the clouds and darkness will be
dispelled.
Sin and doubt will have no place in God's holy Kingdom and the
faithless will be repelled.

We have eyes that see in darkness but we search for God's Holy might.
For in his Kingdom there will never be darkness. There will be no day
or night.

I spoke about the cat that can see in the dark waiting for the morning light.
Through Christ we too can walk through the dark with the help of the flame
of his eternal love. It is a light that will never go out so even when things
seem dark we know that God is standing with us through Christ.

213

The Light

There is a light that shines within me.
I take no credit for it though it is there for all to see.

Its brilliance can be overwhelming causing some to shade their eyes.
Where does this light come from? This is a question I can only
surmise.

There is a light that shines within me.
It is a gift by God the same who created the sea.

The light shines bright and even if I wanted to hide it from others sight.
It would simply glow much brighter, enough to light the night.

The light is the love of Jesus Christ who hung upon a cross for our sin.
The light is the living word of God who came once to die but will come
again.

There is a light that shines within me.
It warms my heart and soul and fills my mind with glee.

God place that light within me while I slept to awaken to find it there.
As long as I allow that light to glow it will lighten every worry or care.

There is a light that shines within me.
I take no credit for it though it is there for all to see.

This gift from God is eternal light and as such will never burn out.
Because the light keeps burning my heart will sing praises without
doubt.

The light is Jesus Christ my Lord, my savior and my friend.
Because of he has helped me find a life where there will be no end.

Okay, I guess I was just killing time. I wrote the next piece because we live in
a period where minutes, seconds and hours are extremely important to us all.
Maybe that is because in this day and age there is so much to do we put a
premium on time. Unfortunately, we let time run us instead savoring each
minute that is given to us. Also, I believe this to be an amusing look at us.

Tick Tock

Tick tock, tick tock. Oh if I could only stop that clock.
My body grows old and my mind does stray.
I forget what I am doing from day to day.

Tick tock, tick tock, I believe I will blame it on that old clock.
If only the darn thing would wind down and stop.
If only the hands would simply stay at the top
They would rotate no more, adding no more seconds, minutes and
hours.
If it would stop my wish would come true. Eternal youth would surely
be ours.

What am I saying? What is it I wish for?
That would mean I would see spring no more.
That would mean no more flowers would bloom and grow.
It would mean I would never feel the summer breezes that blow.

Stop the Clock? Stop the time? What am I thinking with such a hope?
I would have wished for something better if I were not such a dope.
I take back my wish to stop the clocks wondrous movement.
I listen to the ticks, savoring each moment because with time comes
improvement.

Tick tock. Tick tock. I now listen quietly to the sound of the clocks
wondrous sound.
I hear it chime every hour to herald the passing of time where beauty
can be found.

Tick tock. Tick tock. Life is a wonderful collection of hours.
Within it can be found a joy that can truly be ours.

As I wrote the next piece the stories in the news during the past week I have
seen how love can triumph over hatred. I have also seen people who still hate
and it stands between them and true happiness. I won't go into the details
but it has inspired me to write the following.

An Evil Force

An evil force is hatred for it keeps us from understanding.
It stands between each of us and his brother with its passion so
demanding.
An evil force is hatred for true love cannot abide.
In your heart the two of them just simply cannot exist side by side.

What causes this thing called hatred and where does it lead us all.
It leads to war and violence and creates too much noise for us to hear
God's call.
Why do we dwell on this negative force? Why is it that we retain it?
It comes from the very depth of Hell and it will drag us down to the pit.

Hate is a four letter word, my friend as is love, you see.
Love can build bridges but hatred will not allow them be.
The challenge of life is to keep building those bridges back again
And love is a wonderful tool we use so that those bridges we can
maintain.

If we have enough love in our heart we will someday build one giant
span.
It will reach all the way to Heavens gates. If we try we surely can
If not we are condemned to never leave the ground and never know
flights thrill.
Love can lift us off the ground and take our hearts where're we will.

Hatred on the other hand is a heavy weight to bear.
While we carry such a load we find we can go nowhere.
Today is the day for each of us to make a choice between the two.
I choose love and optimism and I pray that you do, too.

This is nothing more than playing around with a very wonderful thought.
Love the Lord thy God with all thy heart and all thy soul and thy entire mind
and love your neighbor as yourself.

L. O. V. E.

Live your life showing compassion to all you meet each day.
You will find that you will reap great joy that way.
Over time you will find you have friends who stay
Through good times or bad whether it is sunny or Gray.

Very often the love that you give will be returned with greater passion.
You have sown the seed and you can watch it will grow in fashion.
Eternal love is given freely by our Lord on high.
It is an emotion which should be shared by you and I.

If you have not noticed the letters L. O. V. E begin every other sentence
of this rhyme.
Put them together and let the love toll bells chime.

Hey guys, have you ever wondered why you wrote that fantasy? Have you ever stopped to think that you created even the villain as well as the hero? I have and it makes me want to search within myself for more reasons. If I am going to write a novel it must have a plot. There needs to be a good guy as well as an adversary. Both of them came from me, the creator. Can you imagine how God feels when he looks at what he has created?

Unfulfilled Fantasies

I wrote a story about a man who stole and robbed banks in the west.
The story told of how he found himself in the afterlife where there was no rest.

I wrote a story about a woman who loved a man to much and compromised her ethics.
One would say her love for him was such that his words to her were edicts.

I wrote a story about people who lived life on the fly.
Now as I look at what I wrote I suddenly wonder why.

Why did I write about a robber and a thief or a woman who loved too much?
Where did these ideas come from and why did I write it as such?

My answer is that within us all there is a rebellious side.
No matter how we try to pretend from this we cannot hide.

So my writing made me dig deep within and scrutinize my heart.
There within my heart and soul is a wilderness from which I cannot depart.

So I write about these things and rightfully I do so.
Each of us knows that temptation follows where ever we may go.

Now I look at my creation and I suddenly realize that I have recreated me.
For it a part of me that they were and are and eventually will be.

The next piece may not be written in an acceptable format. I simply wrote my feelings and tried to make it rhyme. I know life can seem unfair but I also know that if we exercise our faith we can feel better about ourselves. If we dwell on our woes that is all we see. If we look for the silver lining it will appear.

Who We Are

Have you never thought that who we are depends upon who we were?
Have you ever considered that Mom and Dad taught us to call our
elders Ma'am or Sir?

Has it ever occurred to you that old wounds we have can sometimes
leave us lame?
Or that sometimes it becomes an old habit which causes us to find
others to blame?

All these things are part of life and we live them every one.
The secret is to find a way to deal with pain and find joy before our life
is done.
We often find it easier to feel that God has left us down.
We walk through life feeling used and abused meeting each day with a
frown.

It is not God who punishes us or life or Mom or Dad.
It is not our wife or husband or sister and brother that treats us bad.
It is not our children who, after all are only kids today.
It seems your own worst enemy can be yourself who when love calls
will not obey.

Days will come when you find yourself feeling used and abused and
feeling unappreciated.
This is the time when you need to find a way to let unselfish love be
initiated.
Do not blame the world for all your woes or all your pain.
For blame gives nothing and you will find that with it you cannot gain.

Look up for your redemption draweth Nye and your reward is coming
to you.
Follow the Golden rule in everything you say and all you do.

What is Faith to me? It is a wonderful insight into things that are out of
sight. We believe in eternity because there seems to be no alternative. The
Earth has been here for millions of years according to scientists. I can
believe that. It causes me to believe that the very force that created it has
been here even longer. Trust in God and believe in the Word. That is faith.

F.A.I.T.H

Faith is trusting in something that you cannot see
And the ability to envision things unseen and yet can still be.
In all of life is a miracle of life sustained by the power of the Lord.
This is why we read the Bible and why we believe the living word.
Hooray to those who cannot see but still find it easy to believe.

FAITH is the hope that makes us one and all witnesses to his power.
Faith can help us through even the darkest and loneliest hour.
Believe in God and believe also in his only son.
Your reward will come in Heaven when this Earthly life is done.

I was watching TV last night and since the program was not really getting my attention I found myself looking at the rocking chair that my wife and I bought when we were first married. It occurred to me that the chair had been a useful item as we raised three children. I could not help but notice how the years had taken its toll on the old chair just as they had on me. That is why I wrote the following little fairy tale. What if that rocker could talk?

A Rocking Chairs Story

I'm not as young as I once was. My beautiful black luster with golden trim has faded over the years. I sort of remind myself of the master of the house. His hairline has receded and his hair overall has thinned just as the beautiful paint on me has worn, especially on my arms.

When the Master and Mistress purchased me they were newlyweds and I was a brand new piece of furniture. Years have taken their toll. I am not as lustrous as I once was and just like the master my joints are creaking when they rock on me.

The first few years after I was purchased were a piece of cake. I was probably considered more an ornament than anything else. But then he came into my life. A baby boy and now I became a more useful item to the Master and Mistress, although they were now Mom and Dad.

Many a time they would use me to rock him to sleep. Two years later a baby girl followed and now I was really put to work. It seemed like no time had passed before a third child came. The next several years I felt really important.

It was good to be needed but it was tiring and that is when my joints started to creak as they rocked on me. Nobody seemed to mind. It was almost as if I were adding music to the singing which would lure the children to sleep.

Eventually the children grew up and now I was back to being an ornamental piece of furniture. It was a well deserved break but now I was beginning to show signs of age.
This did not bother anyone, though. I truly believe it simply made Mom and Dad more appreciative of my being here. After all, they had spent many hours rocking their little ones to sleep.

Then to my surprise one of those children that Mom and Dad had used me to rock to sleep so many times over the years came home with a child of her own. Mom and Dad became Mamma and Papa. Now there was another child to rock to sleep.

Now, though it was not quite as burdensome. It was not as often and usually during the day. This old Rocking chair that I am can rest at night. Four more grandchildren followed and now the pace picked up. I was used to rock one or the other more often. Once again this was a daytime thing usually and I would sit quietly at night.

As I started to say earlier, my luster is not what it used to be. My joints creak and I probably sing louder now than Mama does. It comes out like, "rickety crack."

I wonder what is next for this old Rocker. Will there be more children? Is there a great place for good rockers in Heaven?

I have seen a lot of changes. I have played a part in the lives of Mama and Papa and each of the kids and grandkids. I must admit that if nothing else comes of it I have had a good life.

Please don't think I'm off my rocker for saying this but I feel like a part of the family.

Not far from where I live is a beautiful state park where there is a waterfall. When you stand looking up you do not see the stream above but it is there. It announces this by sending the water down over the rocks to splash on the rocks below. I watch this and find myself lured into a wonderful state of peace. God created that stream just as he created me. His work is not yet done. I want to help.

Waterfalls

Water rumbling over the falls is rushing to the stream below.
I stand by in the glade watching its rush causing a mist through which
I can see the suns wondrous glow.

The water keeps coming and as it lands upon the stream in constant
and rushing motion
It makes much the same sound as the sea although we are nowhere
near the ocean.

The water keeps coming as it dances at the bottom upon the stones.
The rocks cry out and if you listen you can surely hear their moans.

The stream is a never ending current which keeps rolling downward to
fall.
It almost drowns out natures other sounds including the birds that call.

One cannot see where the water comes from as you stand below
looking above.
It reminds me that there are many things unseen such as Gods eternal
love.

Although we cannot see the water coming we know it is on its way.
This is true of the love of the Son of God who stands with us every day.

So be ye not afraid to believe in things you cannot see.
Though they are unseen this does not mean that they cannot be.

God's love is the living water that sustains life within our heart.
If we accept this living water willingly when his kingdom comes we
shall be a part.

As with that waterfalls there are many things in nature that we cannot
see but we know it is there. You cannot see air but do you doubt its
presence? You cannot see the Holy Spirit but I have no doubt that is exists.

Breathe it in!

Take a breath slow and gentle and let the oxygen fill your lungs.
Now breathe it out with a gentle sigh soft and sweet as any bird has
ever sung.

Now repeat this again and realize that the air you breathe sustains
your life.
Without it your body would not withstand life's cares and strife.

The Holy Spirit is that way, you know.
If you will only let it pass through your heart and soul.

As you breathe it in the spirit feeds the soul within
And as you breathe it out it takes away all strife and sin.

The next breath once more will make you spiritually strong
And as you breathe it out it will carry away all wrongs.

You cannot see the air but you know it is there.
You cannot see the spirit but it is everywhere.

So remember that God has sent this Holy Ghost
So you can live your life to its utmost.

Breathe it in and breathe it out.
The next breath will come, I have no doubt.

God has spoken to many people in the bible using dreams as a mode
of conversation. I am sure he still does. This is a fictional write about a
dream that I never had just as I wrote it but I have had dreams that have
uplifted my soul. I pray you have had them too.

I Once Looked Down

I dreamed that I stood in the air suspended by Gods almighty love.
I could see the shining light from the Heavenly city far above.

I basked my soul in the wonderment as I stood there on that cloud.
From where I stood I saw the beauty and heard the angels singing
sweet and loud.

Then it occurred to me that I knew not what it was that held me there.
I turned my attention to the ground below and suddenly I could only stare.

I fell down from the cloud so high and fell toward the earth below.
I tried to look above again to see Heavens wondrous glow.

But the earths pull was mighty and I fell fast like a rock.
I knew I must pray to God or I would hit the ground with a sudden shock.

"Dear Lord," I prayed. "Please help me for I am helpless and fear that I am lost."
I continued to fall while flying back and forward where ever the winds had tossed.

Suddenly I lay in darkness and wondered why I felt no pain.
I had just fallen from the cloud as fast as a drop of rain.

When I realized that I was at home in my bed and I prayed to My Lord on high.
I wondered what this dream meant. I was sure God was speaking but knew not why.

As I prayed his answer came and replenished my heart with love.
He told me if I would serve him I would focus on things above.

"If you set your mind on worldly things," he said. "They will keep you from rising up."
Focus your heart and soul on Heavenly things and you can share from Christ's own cup.

The earth will go its own way but that direction will lead it to its doom.
There will be hatred, wars and rumors of wars and days filled with gloom.

If you have the spiritual strength to rise above the devastation
Heaven awaits and it is there that you find your revelation.

That is why it is important to keep looking upward toward the city of gold.
Trust in God, allow him to work within your life and be compliant as he works to mold.

If we but confess our shortcomings and learn to love our Master
Heaven awaits our coming and we will be saved from Earths disaster.

It has been so long ago since I first laid my eyes on Ann that it seems almost like a dream. The only reason I know it is not a dream is the fact that we are still together after thirty-seven years as I write this. We have three kids who are now grown and five grandchildren I can rest assured that if this is a dream it has lasted a long, long time.

This is my Valentine to Ann and to you.

Love is never wasted.

I gave my heart and soul to her that day.
My heart broke when she turned away.

I could not let go for my love was strong.
A love like this could not be wrong.

I tried to impress her with conversation
But alas my attempts lead to devastation.

I prayed to God for the right words to say.
I needed to know what would make her stay.

Words are cheap I began to understand.
They come and pass by but rarely land.

I stopped the talk and simply paid attention
To her wants, needs and fears of life's devastation.

Then in silence we both came to know
That our hearts belonged to one another where ever we go.

We found that love can be silent and yet super powerful
As two people join to become one in body and soul.

Now I lay me down to sleep

Comedian Bill Cosby really made me laugh when he used the night time prayer that many parents teach their children as part of his comedy act. Let me see if I can say this right.

Bill: When I was a kid I was taught to pray before going to bed.
"Now I lay me down to sleep. I pray the Lord my soul to keep. If I should die before I wake..." Oh no, I'm not going to sleep tonight.

It went something like that. I laughed so hard I cried because I never understood why anyone wanted to face the prospect of death. When you are eight years old you do not want to think about death. It comes as a thief in the night... along with those monsters that hide under the bed and grab your arms if you do not keep them safely tucked under the covers.

My wife was telling me when she prayed that prayer it came out something like this.

Ifahshodye. All one word which I am sure was her minds way of simply not understanding the concept that death could come while she was asleep. One must wonder what the people who taught their children this prayer were thinking. Was it supposed to be comforting? I suppose they thought so but the average eight year old would probably disagree.

We wanted to think we were going to live forever. Well, I still like the thought. But today I know these old bones are simply going to wear out so I am looking forward to a new body... one that will not know pain. That is my faith.

As a child I preferred songs like "Jesus loves the little children" or "Jesus loves me." My mother's favorite gospel song was, "The meeting in the air." I trust I will meet her there. For those of you who do not know this song it goes something like this.

"There is going to be a meeting in the air in the sweet, sweet bye and bye. I am going to meet you... to meet you over there in that land beyond the sky. Such singing you will hear... never heard by mortal ear, shall be glorious I do declare... and God's own son will be the leading on in that meeting in the air."

That is uplifting and it gives hope. But, "If I should die before I wake?" I still think that is not the prayer for an eight year old. I wonder... what do you teach your kids?

If you listen you can hear his voice. It is sweeter than any earthly sound. It can also be louder than thunder. I have learned to listen while his voice is sweet. The thunder means I have disobeyed.

Higher

"The higher you climb, the harder you fall." That's what Dad would say.
I find that this is true to life as we live from day to day.

He used this in reference to politicians and people who live to succeed.
He always wondered why so many wanted so much more than they need.

There is one time when climbing high is good and I pray I never fall.
I am climbing the stairways to heaven, there to answer my Masters call.

The higher I climb the closer I am to the great protector in the sky.
The closer I am the more strength I obtain. It is his strength I draw from and that's why.

"Why what?" you may ask and I will answer that's why I climb up there.
For the love of the Heavenly Father gives me courage and that's why I dare.

I will climb up higher and higher and pray to God that he holds me firmly in place.
My strength is based on faith and love... his strength and love so that any challenge I can face.

I hear his call and I answer it. "I'm coming Dear Lord," I cry.
I know my love for him comes from him and that is the reason why.

Young love is a passionate thing. The passion will burn out but if you truly one someone you find that when the passion becomes less a factor the intimacy of having a friend who has been with you every step of the way through life becomes more comforting and yes, less demanding. Do not fear love and allow it to grow. Like a seed planted in the ground it is a miracle to watch it grow.

Love in every verse

Boy meets girl and they fall in love.
They gaze at the stars in the heavens above.

He wants to tell her of his warm love in verse
He feels he has the need these words to rehearse.

He gently takes her hand in his and fumbles a bit out a bad case of
nerves.
He feels she is so much more than he really deserves.

He swallows hard and opens his mouth to say, "I love you, my dear."
Shyly and quietly he says the words she longs to hear.

They soon find themselves entwined in one another's arms.
Her lips are sweet... she has auburn hair. He is entranced by her
charms.

He does not know why she returns his advances
With his kisses he worships her... his heart out of great love dances.

Her feelings for him are a reflection of his own.
One day they will be married and shall never be alone.

Their love will grow from infatuation to friendship.
That is why they will stand together even in times of hardship.

Enjoy young love while it is a burning flame
But understand that one day it will not be the same.

The fires will dwindle to a slow burning ember.
But those passionate days will be there to remember.

Let not your love die, but allow it to grow and expand.
Take my word young lovers, one day you will understand.

Happiness! Everyone wants it but we all find ourselves looking for it
in the wrong places. Happiness does come from a series of events. Happiness
is a wonderful ability to see something good coming from any event or series
of events.

Searching

I searched around me but could not find
The one thing I needed... peace of mind.

I searched for it in my occupation
I even search for peace in my nation.

Searching, searching where could it be?
Searching, searching it seemed to be hiding from me.

I looked overseas... I even searched the heavens above.
Finally I realized that peace comes with love.

Love comes from within and not from without.
It is something that is with me if I can only see it, I have no doubt.

After searching and searching I finally surmised
That peace is feeling that can be truly realized

When you look within and accept God's true gift.
The gift that he offers will give your spirit a lift.

Look within yourself and you will see
That peace of mind and happiness will come to be.

Life is funny and the older you get the funnier it gets. One day you find
yourself looking backward more than forward. You find yourself on roads
that you had not meant to go. One day you find that your life has all but
been lived. Prayer and faith is what you live for. Jesus Christ is the provider
of all we need.

Over the Hill

Oh Dear Lord how did I end up here.
I have spent a who life climbing up but I fear
That I at some point must have missed being at the top
Because suddenly I am careening down the hill and cannot stop.

Oh Dear Lord please help me put on the breaks.
I fear that while I was climbing up I made some mistakes.
The biggest one of all is closing my eyes as I struggled to rise.
Oh, Dear Lord when I opened them again I was met with a surprise.

Oh Dear Lord the trip down the other side is wearing out my shoes.
I fear this is not the prize I did chose.
I had planned to reach for your hand at the top
And be lifted to Heaven with you, instead I am over the hill and cannot
stop.

I pray that where ever this road leads me too
I will still be within sight of Heaven and you.
I pray that you know why I am plummeting downward.
I pray that your gracious love will save me, my Lord.

Another of the quips by the famous Will Rogers explained something
that I never really understood until the years went fleeting by. Now I
must admit I find myself chuckling as I read them. I am going to try to
put another one of them to rhyme.

Learn to laugh

A quote from Will Rogers, "If you don't learn to laugh at trouble," he
said
"When you grow old you will have nothing to laugh at, at all."

When I was younger that meant not much to me for I did not see
That the funniest one in the room could easily be me.

Now that the years have passed swiftly by
I now realize Mr. Rogers was telling no lie.

When I look around I see misunderstanding and hate.
If I dwell on these feelings sadness will become my fate.

Therefore I have decided to look for the humor I see.
I will dwell on the laughter to rejuvenate me.

Even if it is myself that makes me smile
I have come to realize that a smile is never out of style.

So take serious the advice of a wise old man
And find humor in whatever form you can.

Laugh and the whole world laughs with you, it's true.
Cry and you cry alone with nobody around for you to cry too.

Words

When I was a kid I would be upset by many of the things my
brothers or my sister... even my school mates would say. My mother
didn't seem to understand my sting. Her favorite saying was, "sticks
and stones can break my bones, but words can never hurt me."

However, though she would recite this she was a perfect example
of someone who could be hurt by words. My Dad could hurt her with a
remark that was maybe not all that much understanding of what she
was going through. Don't get me wrong... Dad was not one to try to
hurt anyone but he was extremely plain spoken.

When I was born my Mom had a really hard labor. I was not
born in a hospital. Not many were in 1945. I was born at home. Dad
was there with her and he stayed with her the whole time.

At one point, though he made a slip. The Doctor looked at him and said, "Well Luke... I bet you would rather be anywhere in the world than here to see this."

Dad shrugged and answered the doctor. "Well it's no worse than pullin' the hook outta the fish's mouth."

My Mom told this to everyone every time she could. As she put it, "I was mad enough to kill that man."

Dad once said he thought the doctor thought the blood and leftovers from my birth were enough to make his stomach queasy. He was simply saying he had seen worse.

Mom had been through an awful lot at that point and Dad's remark would have been better not said.

It is true that sticks and stones can break your bones. However, it is also true that words can leave emotional scars. They can cause anger and this causes rebuttals. One word leads to another and the next thing you know you are in a full scale argument. Two men may even become extremely physical.

Come to think of it... I think I have seen wives throw things at their husbands and it was all because he simply did not use discretion in his choice of words. It may also be that he simply wasn't paying enough attention to what she was saying or her particular frame of mind... or her needs.

You may have seen the commercial where the man is doing something when his wife asks, "Honey, does this dress make me look fat?" He is busy so he simply answers something to the affect of, "yes Dear." The next scene is one husband trying to find a place to spend the night.

Yes, words can hurt. They don't leave scars on your physical body but they can leave scars in your soul.

By the same token, words can be a source healing. That husband in the commercial should have said, "You look beautiful." How many times have any one of us missed the chance to share a healing word with a loved one or a stranger for that matter?

A kind word provokes kindness. Let us all remember that one secret to knowing when that kind word is called for is the ability to communicate with others. Communicate is a two way street. You don't simply talk. You also listen.

When I was a boy my favorite hero was Superman. I imagined flying wherever I wished and I remember wishing that I truly could. That is where this poem came from.

I ride the winds

They come to greet as I go outside.
They have come to take me on a wind swept ride.

The winds are cold but they are also kind.
They refresh my body and calm my mind.

As they push and tug upon me as I walk
I can swear that I hear voices as they talk.

I look up into the sky so blue and see fluffy white the clouds.
They move too and fro as they hover high up above the crowds.

The winds are churning the clouds up high and making the trees below dance.
I stand and contemplate as if I have fallen into a wondrous trance.

However the brisk winds will not allow me to fall asleep.
They instead lift me up far above the ground as if I had made a giant leap.

Now I fly high like a bird lifting far above the ground.
From up in the sky so high the wind is the source of the only sound.

It carries me toward a cloud of white as the wind continues to blow.
As I fly into the beautiful cloud I find it's made of snow.

On and on I ride the winds, floating to and fro in the beauty of the sky.
The wind has shown me what it's like to free as a bird flying high.

Then as I enter into my house once more my imaginative trip is ended.
It was a trip taken within my mind where gravities law can be transcended.

We find ourselves looking for the source of happiness in this world when we should understand that happiness can be enjoyed in this world but the source of that happiness comes from above. We buy insurance policies of all kinds but somehow never know what we pay for until we try to put in a claim and find the insurance company has added exceptions to the coverage and exceptions to the exceptions. WOW! It is over powering.
God does not make it so complicated. Follow him.

Health Insurance

Do you often feel depressed and unhappy?
Do you think your life is just dull and crappy?
Do you find that there is no joy to living?
Do you think there is nothing you have worth giving?

If you answered yes to any of the above
You need to tap into the Masters great love.
It is a health insurance policy like no other.
Your agent is Jesus and he is your brother.

He offers this policy at a price that is affordable.
You only need to give your heart to the lord... in full.
The contract is based on the Ten Commandments.
Follow them and God will issue kinder judgments.

Pray to God and follow is will and you will see
What a wonderful life this can truly be.
The coverage supplied has no exceptions.
There are no deceptions or complications.

Find your agent today... just look for the Lord.
Live you life and follow the word.
The happiness you will know goes beyond this life.
If you keep the faith you can withstand care and strife.

God loves you.....Love him back!

I posted the next one on a website. I thought I would share it here.

Defining Passion

I have been communicating with a friend who mentioned that life without sex seemed dull. It could... I guess! But I wrote a piece which caused him to respond that way. I have been contemplating this and finally decided to create some more discussion.

Let us define passion.

1. A powerful emotion, such as love, joy, hatred, or anger.

Oh my. Passion is a powerful word. It can mean great love, as well as sexual attraction. It can mean a great and wonderful feeling of joy. In my case with my past history of heart problems this would mean a wonderful joy of living. Passion can also be anger or hatred. Well... I guess everything has its dark side. Such a waste. I prefer the joyful kind, myself.

2.
a. Ardent love.
b. Strong sexual desire; lust.
c. The object of such love or desire.

I think I just mentioned sexual desire. That is a wonderful passion. Out of it comes a child who grows up and has passion and creates more children. God said, "Be fruitful and multiply." He didn't mean eat lots of fruit and learn your times tables. When that sexual desire is coupled with ardent love it becomes even more binding hence 'C', the object of such love or desire. When the passion for sex becomes less a factor the passion for the company of a loved one does not. It goes on if the love it strong and true.

3.
a. Boundless enthusiasm: *His skills as a player don't quite match his passion for the game.*
b. The object of such enthusiasm: *Soccer is her passion.*
   Boundless enthusiasm... I guess that is what keeps me writing. I love to put my thoughts, beliefs and fantasies into words. Write them down and share them.

4. An abandoned display of emotion, especially of anger: *He's been known to fly into a passion without warning.*

My Dad had an expression for that. "Don't go flying off the handle," he would say. When I was a kid it was said that I had a temper. I think most kids do. It's how you handle it that counts.

5. Passion
a. The sufferings of Jesus in the period following the Last Supper and including the Crucifixion, as related in the New Testament.
b. A narrative, musical setting, or pictorial representation of Jesus' sufferings.

Now this one is really a strong definition of passion. It takes so many forms. There was great anguish that our Savior bore. He even asked, "If it be possible take this cup from my lips." Why did he follow with, "Yet, not my will be done but yours." That is great love. Maybe it is an example of the greatest love. Painful as it was he had come to fulfill this mission and his passion would not let him turn aside from it.

Here are some more examples of passion:

Synonyms: passion, fervor, fire, zeal, ardor
these nouns denote powerful, intense emotion. *Passion* is a deep, overwhelming emotion: *"There is not a passion so strongly rooted in the human heart as envy"* Richard Brinsley Sheridan.
The term may signify sexual desire or anger: *"He flew into a violent passion and abused me mercilessly"* H.G. Wells.
Fervor is great warmth and intensity of feeling: *"The union of the mathematician with the poet, fervor with measure, passion with correctness, this surely is the ideal"* William James.
Fire is burning passion: *"In our youth our hearts were touched with fire"* Oliver Wendell Holmes, Jr.
Zeal is strong, enthusiastic devotion to a cause, ideal, or goal and tireless diligence in its furtherance: *"Laurie* [resolved], *with a glow of philanthropic zeal, to found and endow an institution for ... women with artistic tendencies"* Louisa May Alcott.
Ardor is fiery intensity of feeling: *"the furious ardor of my zeal repressed"* Charles Churchill. See Also Synonyms at <u>feeling</u>.

Now let me ask you something. What is boring about life if you have a passion for living? The fact is passion and excitement is one and the same. If you can find yourself excited about living day by day you have the greatest gift God can give you while you are still on this Earth.

The only greater passion I can think of is something that must be too great for me to even fully understand now. That would be meeting my

Creator face to face and praising his son for his passion and undying love.

God Bless you all!

Hey Everybody: Yesterday my wife and I went to a birthday party. It was one of my grandchildren's first birthday. It goes without saying that the adults were more excited about his birthday than he was but he did enjoy all the attention. He is one beautiful baby. OK, so I may be just a little prejudiced but doesn't a grandpa have that right?

The following is for him:

You're One today!

I can't believe a full year has passed.
I would have rather it lingered so my time you could last.

I know the next will pass by quickly, too.
I treasure each second, minute, hour or day spent with you.

I cannot find the words to say how much love I feel.
I can only say my love for you is real.

I pray that God will hold you forever in his arms.
It is he who created you and all your charms.

So I wish you a Happy Birthday with all my heart.
And all the love my soul can impart.

Last night we got a snow. We had a few dustings last week. This one was only about two inches but the fact that the temperature has been in the teens for a while meant every single flake that fell stayed right where it landed with more to land on top. The snow came in on an eastbound wind so it moved across the sky. It is a beautiful sight to see. That is why I wrote the following poem.

Snow, Riding the Wind

Snowflakes coming from the sky but they are falling.
They are riding the wind to the side following as they hear it calling.

Snowflakes riding across the darkness... they are small
But they are so many riding in the wind that I could never count them
all.

Snowflakes are dancing in the street lights and landing horizontally.
Because the ground is oh so cold they do not melt away but keep
coming continually.

The beauty of the snow can take your breath and mesmerize you as
you gaze.
It is winter now and the snow has come and will stay for days.

Snow is white and pure, cold and crystallized as it rides the wind.
Oh, the beautiful sight I see when the morning light comes again.

The snow now brightens the day and dresses up the trees.
Now and then it will flow from the branches as it is called by the
breeze.

The snow is a beautiful symbol of the purity of our Lord.
It shines bright and glows in the sun and can fly like a lovely bird.

I was raised in a church that taught that on certain date someone could give
his heart to God and he or she would be saved, sanctified and filled with the
Holy Ghost. I truly believe sanctified...Yes! Filled with the Holy Ghost...
Yes! But even the church I was raised in talked of those who had become
backsliders. If they were saved, how did this happen. I hope you enjoy the
poem. It is meant to be food for thought.

I Am Saved

"I am saved," he cries out loud and clear.
He knows not what he is saved from except his own fear.

"I am sanctified," he yells for all to hear.
He feels consecrated, made holy, purified by the Lord so Dear.

He has promised himself to the Lord... he made a religious vow.
He now feels his eternity with God has been earned somehow.

I will not challenge his right to believe but I challenge him to do
The will of God every day to give social or moral sanction, too.

To whom you may ask? To anyone and everyone.
For sanctification is like a marriage... the trip has just begun.

It is my contention that I have not yet been saved.
But sanctification should be evident in the way I have behaved.

Salvation shall come when I stand before the highest one.
This will come when my Earthly life is lived and done.

What I must do while I work for my Lord
Is to not only recite it but truly live the word.

I will try to live my life with simple humility.
I will, with the help of God purge myself of hate and hostility.

When I stand before the almighty I hope and I pray
I will honestly know what I will be able to say.

"I did not do the right thing to earn my way to heaven with you."
"I served you, my Lord because it was the right thing to do."

The greatest sound I could ever hope to hear from God's only son
Would be come, my friend for your job was well done.

Let's look at LOVE!

Valentines Day is coming. Well, whenever you are reading this,
Valentines day is always coming. So is Christmas, New Year and so on.
They all come once a year. Hey, guys head for the stores now or you'll
be heading for the hill later. Let's look at that dart which Cupid shoots
into the hearts of us all at one time or another. The one which will
make you fall in love. Better... let's look at love. If you have never

looked it up in the dictionary, you may be surprised. This thing called love runs all through humanity.

LOVE: A deep, tender, ineffable feeling of affection and solicitude toward a person, such as that arising from kinship, recognition of attractive qualities, or a sense of underlying oneness.

WOW! Already I am overwhelmed. I love my sister and brother and I still feel the love for my mother and father and my older brother who passed away years ago with just a hint of sadness, however with many wonderful memories. They will always live in my heart.

I fell deeply in love with my wife the first time I laid eyes on her. Those feelings are often called infatuation. The infatuation is a temporary feeling. It will soon be 37 years later and I still love my wife. Now it's a little deeper. Now it is that sense of underlying oneness. She and I have become one and the same.

LOVE: A feeling of intense desire and attraction toward a person with whom one is disposed to make a pair, the emotion of sex and romance.

Those are a glorious part of marriage. Sexual passion by itself, though does not sustain the feeling of love between two people. Once a couple has children they begin to understand just how deep this affection can be. If they share in the responsibility of raising those children they will find it challenging, sometimes scary but extremely rewarding.

LOVE: an intense emotional attachment, as for a pet or treasured object.

What then? I should buy the family cat a valentine? I must admit that I love to sit and watch TV with our cat on my lap but this is not the same kind of love which I feel for my wife and children as well as my grandchildren. It is not the same kind of love that I feel for my brother and sister.

LOVE: A person who is the object of deep or intense affection or attraction; beloved. Often used as a term of endearment. I call my wife 'my love.' Why not? My wife is my love, my beloved. She is a part of me.

LOVE: an expression of one's affection. A strong predilection or enthusiasm. A strong predilection or enthusiasm as well as the object of such enthusiasm.

I love write. You are here you probably do, also. At the very least, you love to read.

LOVE: Christianity Charity.

You've heard of agape love? This is a love given simply because it is good to give.

LOVE: A zero score in tennis.

This seems a far cry from Valentines Day.

LOVE: To have a deep, tender, ineffable feeling of affection and solicitude toward a person or persons.

We feel this for our husbands and wives... mother and father... sisters and brothers... our oldest and best friend. But this word love can be a deep thing or a very shallow desire or want.

The list goes on and on. What a powerful word love is. I once saw a church bulletin board with this slogan. "Love is a four letter word." I think we should use it more.

Finally and of course I could not end this without one last definition:

LOVE: Eros or Cupid.

Happy Valentines Day.

When I was young I loved the hot summer day. I never quite liked the cold although I did enjoy making snowmen and snow angels. As I have grown older I find I do not handle either well. I guess that is why I wrote the following.

Shivers

February can seem bleak... cold and unforgiving.
I wear three layers of clothes and still find myself shivering.

I can hardly wait for the onset of spring.
When I will see the first rose bud and hear the birds sing.

However, for now I am cold all the way to my fingertips.
I have a runny nose and dry, chapped lips.

Oh how I long for warmer weather to embrace me.
I await a soft warm breeze and spring flowers to see.

However, the man says we may soon get more snow.
With the snow come strong cold winds that blow.

I wait for the spring flowers but I know I must wait.
I am reminded that spring does come on this date.

Everything has its purpose and that includes snow and sleet.
I have seen the seasons recycle themselves many times and repeat.

The spring is followed by the heat of the summer.
Then comes the autumn when trees drop their leaves and start to slumber.

The trees fall into their state of dream the winter comes on.
We endure another cold season until it is gone.

The wonder of it all is again blooms the spring Dogwood.
I would hold onto the spring if only I could.

Since I cannot I will simply accept each day that I live.
For each day I live has something to give.

As a kid I would often have dreams like this one. Christmas came and went and I slept through it. It is ironic that St. Valentines Day comes at a time of year when the only flowers available are hot house flowers. Wouldn't it be wonderful if it came in the spring when the hills were in full bloom? I guess it works out, though. Easter comes at that time of year. Everything is in the process of being reborn just as our Lord and Savior was reborn.

The Plight of the Dogwood

A cold and snow filled February day was proclaimed Valentines Day.
People will give roses and chocolates and send cards and letters all of
which say
I love you my Dear ones... I love you every one and all on this
wonderful day.

Alas, the Dogwood will never know this day for it slumbers beneath the
snow.
The stories of love and of cupids piercing arrow are stories she will
never know.
When the Dogwood awakens and her blossoms come and spring melts
away the snow

Valentines Day will have passed and gone, missed by the Dogwood for
another year.
I will save a special kiss, a token held by my heart for this friend so
dear.
I will wait until she is awake and say with a loving voice that is soft but
clear.

Though you slept through the day that we all celebrate as a day of
jubilation
I have saved the feeling to share with you so you can join in the
celebration.
As I watch your blossoms grow and unfold I will pray with great
elation.

You have renewed yourself one more time to rejoin me and for this I
thank the Lord.
It is true that the dogwood symbolizes the greatest love... the love of
God's only son.
It is true that when I see her blossoms in bloom I celebrate for life has
again begun.

The Dogwood blossoms hold a memory of a love which death could not
defeat.
Each year she is born... lives and dies to be born again, a life to repeat.
She is an annual reminder that Christ died on the cross but death
could not hold him.
He died for us but he lives again, we sing of it with every Easter hymn.
For God so loved the world that he gave his only begotten Son that
whosoever believeth in him should not perish but have everlasting life.

Are you tired of these poems about snow yet? I have written many of them. I am embracing the oncoming spring but I must admit I am always fascinated with the snow. March is an interesting month. It can be warm, windy, snowy... even rainy. One thing is not is boring.

Snowbound

Once more I sit inside my window
Watching the flakes of snow that flow.

They ride the March winds but slowly sink to the ground
Where they join others with nary a sound.

The ground is white and the sky is gray.
The snow is the only thing that brightens the day.

It dances and waves, it swirls and it curtsies as to the ground it falls.
Once it lands upon the ground the wind moves it here and there as if it crawls.

This is called a Robin show for it will not last for long.
It is nature's last taste of winter as the March winds sing their song.

I watch the snow and find myself mesmerized by its constant flow.
Soon April will come with spring showers that will wash away the fallen snow.

Don't we all find ourselves wondering if we have the ability to serve God, to love one another? Don't we many times get to feeling that there are too many unanswered questions? Are we ever tempted to give up on our most precious dreams? I believe we all face days like that. I also believe that our Heavenly father knows about our doubts as well as our faith. He applauds our faith and forgives us our doubts if we but lay them upon his shoulders.

Climb all the way:

I climbed the mountain halfway to the top.
There I almost decided to stop.

For the journey from this point onward would wear me out.
To say the least I had many things to doubt.

The voice of God kept urging me on.
Once you've started, he said don't quit till your done.

Now that you are halfway to the summit of the mountain
You are so much closer to the holy fountain

Wherein there lies the living water for the spirit.
The wind you hear is Angels singing, you've but to open your heart to
hear it.

Keep climbing all the way to the mountain peak.
You will find there the answers that you now seek

From the top of the highest snow cap you will reach Heavens door.
Is that not what you came this far for?

Climb, my friend and let not doubt dissuade.
I will not allow your wonderful dreams to fade.

As you read from John 4:4-26 you realize that there were separations in the days of Jesus just as there are today. Jews did not associate with Samaritans. The woman at the well did not understand how it was that Jesus, being a Jew would even speak to her let alone ask for a drink. This was one more opportunity for the Master to share the word with anyone who would accept it.

The Woman at the well:

At a town called Samaria Jesus sat down by a well for he was tired.
He was thirsty and asked a Samaritan woman for a drink to which she
enquired,
"You are a Jew and I am a Samaritan; how is it you ask me for a
drink?"

Jesus said, "If knew the gift of God and knew who asked you for this
drink.
You would have asked him for living water to drink and find they
thirst no more."

The woman knew not what he meant and asked, "Lord where this
living water is stored?"
Jesus answered her, "he who drinks from this well will find they thirst
again
But he drinks of the water I speak off will feel it wash away their sin."

I ask you friend would you join me as we drink to God's only Son?
Drinking of his holy water until our life on Earth is done.

Early one week in March we shut down the furnace and opened the
windows at night. The temperature was in the 70's and 80's. Before long
the furnace was running, the windows and doors were closed and it was
snowing again. Even so, it is beautiful to watch the snowfall.
Everything about life is beautiful if we only have eyes to see.

Consider the Beauty

Consider the sky as it changes colors and shades to let us know
When we can expect the rain, sleet, hail or snow.

Consider the clouds which also reflect the changing weather.
They can be fluffy white or gray or sometimes both together.

Consider the snowflake which drifts to the ground.
One makes no matter but watch as thousands come down.

As they all flow downward together deflecting the light
They turn the gray sky to a sky of white.

Consider the flowers dressed in red, yellow, gold and blue.
I have watched them dance in the field as the spring breeze blew.

Consider the tree as it dresses itself for the coming of spring.
It is fully dressed for summer, wearing many shades of green.

Consider that same tree as she dresses up for autumn's arrival
And then prepares herself for winter... she is an icon of survival.

Consider all the creation, man is a part all of which by God is blessed.
Consider the God given ability to see past the mountains in the west.

See life in all its glory and know we are but a part of something far
greater.
From the tiniest seed to the volcano's great crater.

Consider the beauty of the butterfly feeding on a flower so bright.
She takes only its nectar and spreads seeds of delight.

Consider how each creature offers something to the balance of life.
It seems we are all married to one another; yes we are as husband and
wife.

Ask not

If you are like me you have been watching the news and the more you see the less you want to see. We are fighting with global warming but nobody wants to admit it. We are fighting with other nations and even worse; we are fighting amongst ourselves.

I am going to ask you to stop thinking like a Republican or a Democrat but as a citizen of the greatest Country on Earth. Consider what is happening to us. We are forgetting many of the things our founding fathers stood for. We are divided on many issues from Social Security and Health Insurance to the war in Iraq and the tensions between our government and that of Iran.

I want us to step back for a moment. The problems in the world will still be there when we return but maybe we will be more able to consider who we are and what we stand for in the United States of America.

It has been said, "A nation divided against itself cannot stand." I think we need to scrutinize ourselves. This starts with our President, our congressmen; both Federal and state.

I read once that Democracy would work until someone finds out how to use it for his own selfish purpose. We have performed a bit of a miracle. After two hundred years we are still here and we are still a Democracy. It's that 'selfish' thing that worries me.

John Kennedy once said in a speech, "Ask not what your country can do for you. Ask what you can do for your country." I thought it was noble at the time. As I grow older and see young men going off to die for this country it makes me wonder if those lives will not be lost in vain.

We should all live by the late President Kennedy's words. But that is the clincher. We should all: If those who have sworn to serve the people use their position for their own selfish reasons how can they possibly expect us to follow like stray dogs?

Man is inherently selfish by nature. Christ knew that. He spoke of it many times. He also knew that much of what we are living through today was coming. I have friends who say, "Don't worry. He's coming soon. These are the last days Jesus predicted."

These are indeed the last days but we know not how long a day is to God. Jesus once said a day to God lasts a thousand years. If you do not believe in Christ or God then I would suppose it is easy to eat, drink and be merry for tomorrow you die. However if you do believe consider this.

What if Christ came tonight and found us simply sitting and waiting. It's sort of like the servants the master gave the talents too. Those who put their talents to work were found worthy. Those who buried theirs so they would not lose them were rebuked by the master.

Getting back to the good ole' USA, I can only say that if we are going to survive as a country we all have to put a lid on those selfish desires and start working together. This is important from the very poorest to the very richest.

I would challenge those multi-million dollar oil companies to start considering the prospect of investing some of their millions in some other source of power. I would challenge each of us to use as little power as possible as a way of saying, "We care."

Our nation is just like a chain fence. It can only be as strong as the weakest link. Those who have the power have to consider the possibility that their power will mean nothing if we fall under the weight of our own corruption. It happened to the great Roman Empire. If we aren't careful it could happen to us.

Let us put partisan politics away for good. We are all American's. There is no I in TEAM! Are we willing to become a team once more? We should our might many times in the past. The challenge is far greater today.

I had a wonderful and restful night last night. This is not always the case. There have been nights when I finally got up and booted up the computer for I realized I was not going to sleep, simply toss and turn. This night, though was restful and seemed so short for sleep is like that. That why I penned the next poem.

Under the Cover

I lie under the cover of darkness and count the seconds as they go by.
I allow my mind to drift lazily into the wonderful state of euphoria in
which I lie.

My mind is focused on nothing; nor does it want to be.
It has been a long busy day and my thoughts only want to be free.

I lie under the cover of darkness and hear only the sound of the night.
As I relax I hear my own breath with eyes closed for they want no light.

Soon soft dark clouds will envelope me and I will drift off to wondrous
sleep.
I have prayed to my God to watch over me as into the dark cloud I
creep.

I lie under the cover of darkness; a wonderful journey I will take.
My body relaxes and my senses are dull and I enter a dreamless state.

This time of rest is God's gift to me and my dreams are quiet and kind.
They are made up as a composition and processed by my own mind.

I lie under the cover of darkness but I am not unaware of its existence.
As I am carried off into dreamland my mind gives no resistance.

Sleep, oh body and mind and let the Spirit rest, too.
Let this wonderful state of rest last the whole night through.

Paul wrote in second Corinthians the following. To read it all to Chapter
4:7-12.
But we have this treasure in jars of clay to show that this all-surpassing
power is from God and not from us. We are hard pressed on every side, but
not crushed; perplexed, but not in despair; persecuted but not abandoned.

Persecution is Proof

We carry the sorrow that Jesus has died
But we also show forth a light that we should not attempt to hide.

His death paid the price for the sins of man
Sins of yesteryear and also today for he does understand.

We are hard pressed but we are not crushed.
We are perplexed but our praises to him are not hushed.

We are struck down but we are not annoyed
We carry the body of Jesus till he returns because his forgiveness we
have enjoyed.

The power of God will lift our souls high when our mortal body has
died.
We shall sup with our lord and with him abide.

Eternity will be our fate and joy with no end.
This is why we have faith that no one can offend.

March is a strange month. It turns from winter to spring and back to winter
and then spring returns again. I keep hoping it is here to stay this time. It
inspired me to write about the renewal of life. The wonderful balance of
nature is built upon the fact that each part works to complete the whole. I
hope you enjoy this next poem.

Flutter by

The March winds are now coming soft and slow.
The warmth of the sun is melting the snow.

The snow turns to water and seeps into the ground.
It will water the flowers and now I hear a familiar sound

It is the sound of birds singing in the air as they build their nest.
They take little time now to stop and rest.

I see the sprouts of the daffodils as they reach for the sun.
They will grow and blossom until they are done.

They are crying out now to a dear friend.
If you listen carefully you can hear the message they send.

Flutter by little butterfly and drink of the nectar we share with you.
We know you need us and we need you, too.

Your wings are a beautiful sight admired by all.
We will welcome your presents till the coming of fall.

The wild flowers in the fields and the buds on the trees
Call for your presence as they wave in the spring breeze.

Flutter by little butterfly for we beg for your presence.
Caress our petals and we will share our essence.

Flutter by little butterfly for you share life with each flower and tree.
We are all a glorious part of life's reverie.

It's a warm day in spring

On a warm and beautiful spring day there in the southwest looms a
dark cloud.
As I look upon it from afar I see it churning and hear thunder though
it is not yet loud.

The sun still shines but it will soon relent as the clouds move closer to
take command.
As they do this I see lightning streaks and the thunder now rumbles all
across the darkened land.

Then comes the rain and it does not come softly but falls as if the cloud
strikes with light, sound and rain.
The wonder of this majestic show is that the cloud moves on for it has
not long to reign.

As it passes overhead and sends the raindrops along with lightning and
the thunder
It causes one to stop and wonder.

What force creates the changing weather by which all of life is
sustained?
One must admire the power of the life giving storm for the life I speak
of it does maintain.

I see the lightning and I hear the thunder; I also feel the raindrops fall.
They are all a part of Gods creation; the rain, trees and also flowers'
all of life both large and small.

Have you ever found yourself watching the news and feel like you
want to yell angry thoughts at the news man or one of our politicians? I
have. I shouldn't but I do become angry when they seem more content to
fatten their bank accounts than to make the world a better place for our
grandchildren to grow up in. The sad part is when I speak in anger I have
profaned myself. The world will go its own way but if we believe in Christ
we will follow him.

He Hears

Even during times when my faith doth wane and my voice is soft and
weak
He hears my cries and reaches forth his arms and asks me what I seek.

Even when my anger is controlling what I do and say
His love forgives and he gently leads me back on the right way.

Even when I let my passions rule and do not follow his loving lead
He sends Angels to guide me from my selfish ways and back to the
Lord I need.

Even when I prove myself to be a sinner and weak in spirit
My Heavenly father calls to me with a voice the echoes so I hear it.

He is love, patience and my guiding light through a world that goes
astray.
He calls to me, "come home, my child for you need my light today.

When I speak in anger to a brother or sister he hears that too.
He quietly urges me to speak not in passion and shows me what to do.

His fury is enough to scare me and to make me learn to fear
But his love is soft and comforting and something that I hold dear.

Serve the Lord for he is our maker and truly is our Father in Heaven
above.
If we will but listen to him he will teach us how to love.

Keep silent and let me speak; then let come to me what may. Why do I put myself in jeopardy and take my life in my hands? Though he slay me, yet will I hope in him; I will surely defend my ways to his face. Indeed, this will turn out for my deliverance. Job 12:13

It is good for us to be reminded that even Jobs patience began to wear thin. We often find ourselves wondering why the Lord allows death, destruction, devastation and pain. My father once said, "Show me a man with calluses on his hands and I will show you a man who never worked hard. I guess all of life is a test to see how spiritually strong we are.

Let Me Speak

Any man who has ears
I pray that he hears
For the words I say will be my vindication.
I know the Lord and will follow him and this will be my salvation.

A mans Earthly life wastes away quickly; his youth is not eternal.
Man born of woman enjoys a short life which sometimes seems like an
infernal.
He springs up like a flow and then he simply withers away.
A mans life in the eyes of God does not even last a day.

The spirit of man is like unto a tree which can be cut down and thrown
aside
But it will renew itself and grow once more and with the Son abide.
Like a mountain which erodes and crumbles or as water wares a stone
away
God's power and lustrous majesty will return the life of a man who will
obey.

I think sometimes we get caught up in a form of worship that consists of reciting psalms and singing praises but do not pay enough attention to the true gift given us by our Heavenly Father and his son our Lord, Jesus Christ. Jesus performed miracles to get our attention but he knew from the beginning that his destiny was to hang on that cross and he know he would have to defeat death to make a true point to man. He did!

Have you performed a Miracle?

My friend, have you performed a Miracle today?
I am guessing I know what you are about to say.

It is one thing for a man to teach what he claims is true
But it is another thing to demonstrate it to me and you.

That is why the miracles of Jesus are a vital part
The miracle was winning over the sinful heart.

For he not only spoke of Gods' great might.
He came to show us the majesty of his great light.

His miracles were a message to those far and near
That the son of God was truly here.

Yet, man rejected his wonderful works and cast them aside.
Gods' goodness was too brilliant and we all tried to hide.

They hung our Lord upon the cross and mocked him and jeered.
His purity had caused man to run from his love for they found that
they feared.

They feared the responsibility of admitting their sins and weakness.
They could not bear to bough down before him in meekness.

The final Miracle the Son of God did impart
Was a gift given to us all, given by Jesus from his heart.

He hung on the cross and prayed for our forgiveness.
He arose from the dead so that his disciples would bare witness

That god so loved the world that he gave us his son.
This is why Jesus proclaimed to the Father, "thy will be done."

This next piece is inspired by not one but five grandchildren; all of which I love and cherish. The first years of a Childs' life are so wonderfully pure. Maybe that is why Jesus said, "except ye be as little children you cannot enter the Kingdom of Heaven.

The Power of Innocence

He knows not what power he holds in those tiny hands.
He has no idea of the joy his gaze can impart as before you he stands.

He seems only to know that you love him and he loves you purely from
the heart.
The joy is a part but only the start of the greatest exchange of love that
life can impart.

He is just over one year of age and knows not what the world around
him holds in store.
He knows but simple joys derived from your hugs and kiss; smiles and
more.

He provokes you to love him without condition or restriction.
One may even call it a love caused addiction.

He is my grandson and his smile is the light of my life.
His chatter is like music which wipes away all of life's strife.

He does not know that he makes me feel strong and tall.
His love is pure and it creates a wonderful crevice into which I gladly
let myself fall.

No matter what I am doing, I never mind stopping to respond to his
gaze
For this is the joy we share during these wonderful days.

We should never outgrow this innocent love which he knows.
Alas, one day he will, I fear the path I followed is the one down which
he now goes.

Typical of March, as I write this the sky is gray again today. I don't mind. It's still warm enough that we have the house open and the heat off. Spring will bring showers but that will help things grow and should be embraced as a part of the flow of nature. That is why I wrote the following poem.

Look for the Sunshine

It's so typical of this time of year; the sky is dark and gray.
However I will not look upon the sky with great dismay.

If I look I see the sun is shine even on this cloudy day.
Its rays may be filtered by the clouds that roll overhead today.

If one has the insight to realize it he sees the sun even in a raindrop.
It may rain today; it may come quickly and just as quickly stop.

When the rain has done its part the sun will shine in skies of blue.
It shines with rays of warmth and light and smiles at me and you.

Let not the gray skies bring you pain for they are a part of natures
flow.
Mix the raindrops with the sun and trees and flowers will grow.

My Dad was not a wealthy man but he gave each of his children as
well as my wife all the love we needed and I praise God for that. Many
fathers do not realize that they hold the capacity to build their children up or
tear them down. The mistakes of the parents are often the cause of the
problems of many young men and women who grow up feeling that they are
not worth being loved. Let's try to show them that God loves them. We love
them, too!

Sins of the Fathers

He never had a father who cared for him as a father should.
He wasn't kind, forgiving or ever showed that he understood.

Therefore he did not have a male figure to look up too.
Instead his father was a man to fear; he never felt he pleased him no
matter what he might do.

When he grew up and found that he was soon to be a father to a new
baby boy
He felt that the child was a problem, someone who would only serve to
annoy.

He did not learn from his father so he did not impart love to his son.
What started with the forefathers would be devastating by the time it
was done.

His son felt unloved, unworthy of being loved and that he was of no
use.
He realized not that he was a sad product of a father's horrid abuse.

He, like his father before him was a victim of the forefathers oversight.
That is why he got a gun and tried to rob a store one night.

It would not end happy and it ended in his death at an early age.
The sins of the fathers were passed to the son and his life was the wage.

Mourned only by his mother, he lay dead in the grave.
It would have taken only the love of his father for his life to be saved.

I wrote the next piece on the day before April 4th. and my wife and I will celebrate the end of our thirty-seventh year as man and wife. I don't know about you but I think she deserves a medal of some kind.

First you Fall in Love

This is something every young man should learn.
He usually doesn't find it out until the years have taken their turn.

First you fall in love with the girl who is so sweet.
It is a fall so once you've fallen there is no retreat.

You learn to know her day by day.
You learn to love her; come what may.

You find that you eventually fall out of love.
You begin to feel an emotion which is far above.

She becomes the one with whom you share your every thought.
If this has not happened your love goes for naught.

You find she is the source of your strength and power.
She is beside you even as you go through your darkest hour.

She is encouragement, love, tender kiss and more.
Her sleepy sigh is enough to make your soul lift and soar.

It all starts with a feeling of physical attraction.
It will grow strong enough to withstand any distraction.

The day will come when what you truly want from your love so dear
Is the knowledge she still holds you near.

This kind of love, time cannot erode.
It becomes a spiritual strength to help you carry the heaviest load.

Our Dogwoods Earthly struggle is over. We had a major plumbing problem and in order to fix that the front yard had to be completely dug up and replaced. That meant after the wonder Dogwood tree which had our friend been since before our marriage began is gone. The following poem is a eulogy. It may sound silly but it is a reminder that there really is no end to life.

Goodbye Old Friend

You decorated our every spring with pink blossoms so beautiful.
You stood proudly throughout many storms when skies were dull.

You turned your colors in fall to an exquisite color of ruby red.
Once we had given you up for dead.

My friend, you fought your way back and once more tried to grow.
We know that all earthly life is temporary but we hate to see you go.

I am sure that if there is room for Dogwood trees in Gods kingdom.
He will find a place for you to grow and bloom; where you will be
welcome.

I believe you will bloom in pink as in spring and as your blossoms float
away
You will stand tall and proud for eternity and a day.

When the leaves turn ruby the beauty will be greater than they have
ever been.
When they fall away the blossoms will return and the cycle will start
again.

I believe there is no winter in Heaven so you will eternally be free.
To show off your wonderful colors for all the Angels to see.

www.ingramcontent.com/pod-product-compliance
Lightning Source LLC
Chambersburg PA
CBHW050407260626
47156CB00003B/913